HE REJOICES OVER ME

A Story of the Life, Lessons and Love
of Crystal Marie Skula

By Nicholas J. Skula Jr.

Creative Force Press

Creative Force Press

He Rejoices Over Me
© 2013 by Nicholas J. Skula Jr.
www.HeRejoicesOverMe.com

This title is also available as an eBook. Visit
www.CreativeForcePress.com/titles for more information.

Published by Creative Force Press
4704 Pacific Ave, Suite C, Lacey, WA 98503
www.CreativeForcePress.com

Scriptures quoted in this book are taken from the King James Version.

ISBN: 978-1-939989-06-2

Printed in the United States of America

Photo credits: the Skula Family

"Nick & Beryl,
Thank you for allowing me the blessing of reading
the manuscript of your book. I was so deeply
touched by its content. Each chapter was filled
with interesting life-stories and hope and faith and
rich insights. It made me laugh and cry – I was so
blessed by Crystal's life and faith. The final
chapters dealing with your grieving process and a
journey to heaven was so touching and helpful. I
believe many will be encouraged and blessed by
this redemption story."

– Gary Zarlengo, Senior Pastor of Smithtown
Gospel Tabernacle, Long Island, New York

He Rejoices Over Me, by Nicholas Skula, is a book for this generation. It is a unique writing about a young girl's dreams and aspirations. Crystal Skula was ahead of her time. She marched to the beat of her own drum. She was young, beautiful and popular, yet at the same time, humble, which connected to the hearts of many young people.

Personal testimony and pictures by Crystal's friends will commemorate the authenticity of this book. Cancer survivor from stage four cancer for several years, literally thousands of Christians were praying for a miracle on Crystal's behalf. This ballerina story will be a comfort to any parent going through this. It's a fascinating read that will have you turning the pages.

Many who read excerpts found themselves in tears. You cannot help but get drawn into this story. Just the way Crystal faced her death, losing her battle with brain cancer, her school friends were deeply moved. Three years later, they asked Crystal's parents to speak at what would have been Crystal's high school graduation. Crystal's mother was presented with a high school ring and a diploma.

This book was six years in the making, and if there ever was a time to write about a family losing a child, it is now. The story is a blend of beauty, faith, courage, hardship, and victory. It has a supernatural ending that will leave every reader believing and rejoicing.

TABLE OF CONTENTS

ACKNOWLEDGEMENTS

I would like to personally thank the following:

God the Father
Holy Spirit the Comforter
Jesus the Savior
Amy Berkitt
Audrey Anderson
Awana Club of Patchogue Baptist Church
Brother Anthony Ray
Carol, Tony & Marissa Barrasso
Casey Skula
Christ Tabernacle Security Team
Christ Tabernacle Choir
Christine, Nicholas & Samuel Rugeris
Deb Paprocky
Dee Anderson
Professor Denise Miller
Marissa Miller
Dr. Doug, Dr. Sheila & Alana Foerth
East Islip Health & Fitness
Erin & Casey Meade
Mr. & Mrs John & Marge Goehring
Friends of Karen,
Give Kids the World, Kissimmee Florida
Jeanette Olish
John & Elizabeth Petty
Chaplain Juan & Adriana Pichardo
Kerry Farnum
Kristin Cieciroski
Kristy Roman
Late Rev. Calvin Hunt & Miriam Hunt
Lisa Anschlowar
Make A Wish Foundation
Megan Mohr
Michelle & Louie Hernendez

Ms. Jean Baker
Moms-In-Prayer International
Mother's Kiss
Mr. & Mrs. Benjamin & Maribell Gonzalez
Mr. & Mrs. Gary Rado, Debbie & A.J.
Mr. & Mrs. Jerome & Marion O' Grady
Mr. & Mrs. John & Aggie Contes
Mr. & Mrs. John & Toni McKearnan
Mr. & Mrs. Kevin & Nancy Sheehan, Kevin Jr & Kayla
Mr. & Mrs. Marco & Tanya Salazar
Mr. & Mrs. Nicholas & Eleanor Skula SR
Mr. &. Mrs. Sam & Nancy Maldonado
Mr. & Mrs. Scott & Carol Forsmith
Mr. & Mrs. Anthony & Carol Trocchia
Mr. Norm Devanu
Mrs. Barbie Alavelse
Mrs. Eileen Dougherty
Mrs. Eileen Kogurt & Shea Kogurt
Mrs. Joann McKeon
Pastor Steve & Mrs. Mary Carey
Pastor Angelo & Sophie Mena
Pastor John & Evelyn Rivera
Pastor Frank Lorenzo
Pastor Gary & Mrs. Diane Zarlengo
Pastor Michael & Mrs. Maria Durso
Pastor Rob & Mrs. Catherine Thorne
Pastor Salvatore & Josie Greco
Pastor Stephen Willoughby
Plainedge Baptist Church
Teruyuki Higa
Okinawa Kenpo Karate-Do Association
Smithtown Christian School
Smithtown Gospel Tabernacle
The Care Bears & The Jr. Church Dept.
The Just Kidz Ministry
Tom & Stacy Costanza
Wendy Silva
Yorktown Rotary Club of Virgina

FOREWORD

Many people come and go out of our lives, but every once in a while, if we are lucky, we meet someone who has a lasting impact on us. Rarer still is meeting someone who will change the way we view and live our lives forever. The Skula family has had that kind of profound impact on my life.

When I accepted my first teaching position at Smithtown Christian School, I knew I was in for a tremendous growth and learning experience. Little did I know that the most valuable lessons in my life were going to come from an 11-year-old little girl, who taught me more about love, grace, faith and true courage than I could ever have learned in life otherwise. Crystal was in my very first class and immediately stood out to me. She was an extremely quiet, petite young lady, and yet there was an intense competitive spirit about her.

I will always remember field day, watching in amazement as this shy young lady rounded the bend of the 1/4 mile run event with a quarter of a track lead. This fighting spirit and strength would serve her well in life. To my delight, I was assigned as a sixth grade teacher the next year, which positioned me to stand alongside the Skula family as the events unfolded that would change all of our lives forever. I was repeatedly challenged in my walk with the Lord as I observed what true strength of faith in action looked like in the Skula family.

I remember the day I learned of Crystal's diagnoses. I was watching my 5-year-old play soccer, and as a parent my heart broke for Beryl, Nick and Nick III. Upon leaving the field, I immediately went to the hospital to see them, wanting to bring some support to the family. I prayed all the way for God to give me the words to comfort them, but having no idea what I was going to say. What I found upon entering the hospital room was strength, faith and a trust in God that was beyond words. That day, as I left the hospital, I was the one feeling comforted and uplifted. The word of God says to come to him with a childlike faith. I truly feel I understand what that means now as I watched Crystal face challenges that would terrify even the most mature adults. She faced death without fear, but with a true trust in her God and that all His promises were true.

We all struggle with difficult situations at different times in our lives. Through this beautiful family, I have learned some of life's most precious lessons. Their example has truly changed me and the way I live my life. I know their story of incredible faith, grace and trust in God will impact you as you read this book. The Skula family knows how to love and how to make you feel loved. Even when they are in the midst of personal crisis, they have a way of making others feel important, and always point the way back to God. They are a shining example of what a true Christian walk should be.

Crystal truly embodied the verse in 1 Timothy 4:12: *"Don't let anyone look down on you because you are young, but set an example for the believers in speech, in conduct, in love, in faith and in purity."* For me, the teacher became the student, and the student taught purely by example.

Debbie Paprocky

Crystal's 6th grade teacher and Nick and Beryl's eternal friend.

INTRODUCTION

In today's world with so few Godly role models, the Holy Spirit compelled my wife and I to write this story about our daughter, Crystal. As her parents, we of course wanted the very best for our only daughter and encouraged her to live her life for Jesus Christ. At an early age, she made a conscious decision to receive Him not only as Savior, but as her Lord, and to be faithful to God. We needed to tell the world that her Creator remained very much involved as a part of Crystal's life journey and struggles, and *that* made her an overcomer.

People would ask, "What was the secret in Crystal's upbringing?" We referred them to the Gospel letters in the Bible: **B**iblical **I**nstructions **B**efore **L**eaving **E**arth.

We all hope to find joy in being faithful to God in all things during our spiritual journeys. When life seems not worth living, remember this: a mighty God in Heaven loves you. He *is* Love (1 John 4:8). All the hairs on your head...He's counted (Matthew 10:30). The tears you cried are all bottled up and held by God (Psalm 56:8). He sacrificed His own Son so you can live (John 3:16). He awaits our coming home to be reunited with Him. So precious in His sight is the death of His saints (Psalm 116:15).

He desires to bring His family together that have been separated by the two kingdoms, Heaven and Earth. Gifts and new homes await those who believe and follow His only begotten Son (Isaiah 40:10 and John 14:2). Sickness and disease have been abolished in the new realm called Heaven (Revelation 21:4), a place He created (Genesis 1:1). He offers every one eternal life there (John 3:16).

There are two ways of looking at your life. The first is the natural way; what the world calls "normal." It makes sense, but the way our family chose to live is the greater way; the supernatural way of God. When things you don't understand seem impossible to change, like a flood, the Spirit of God lifts up a standard against the enemy who seeks to destroy you (Isaiah 59:19). Nothing is impossible with God (Luke 1:7-13). He is the greatest reason for living.

Your connection with God starts through prayer in order to bring His intimate presence (Romans 10:8-9).

Throughout *He Rejoices Over Me*, you will see the handprint of God. He inspired me to write from my heart and be very transparent. The story is just another modern day miracle God allowed us to see and take part in. Through studying His awesome love for His earthly children, I learned how to be a good father on earth to my own children, Crystal and Nicholas III.

1

A LOVE FROM HEAVEN

"Many waters cannot quench love, neither can the floods drown it: if a man would give all the substance of his house for love, it would utterly be contemned."
–Song of Solomon 8:7

Crystal Marie Skula was born on November 23, 1991. Although the day was cloudy, she was a bright ray of sunshine in our lives. Crystal was always independent. Her first words were "I do! I do!" She always wanted to be first in everything and never liked second best.

Since the age of seven, Crystal was privileged to attend a Christian school. One day after returning home, she told us the teacher asked if any children would like to accept Jesus Christ as their Savior. Crystal prayed with her teacher, Ms. Baker, and we were thrilled. Her love for the Lord grew strong. After being baptized several years later, she wanted to help her Mom and Dad and her brother Nicky in the junior church.

Crystal blossomed into a lovely young girl, tall, slender and blonde. Although her appearance would light up a room when she walked in, she didn't feel comfortable in her skin. When people would compliment her, she always blushed. After really getting to know Crystal, you discovered that her real beauty was inside. She wasn't shy about showing her real God-given gift.

God blessed and favored her life with a never-ending journey of new relationships. To really understand Crystal, you have to know her parents.

We're two people with opposite personalities—me, her father, masculine and authoritative; her mother, a lady, feminine in all her ways. Once Beryl became a mother, her affection was focused on her children. Her biggest task was dividing her love between Nicholas and Crystal.

After enduring a lot of dating and failed romances, I just couldn't find that special person for me. There was a popular country western song back in the day that said *looking for love in all the wrong places*...that described my life in search of that special one. The age of 30 was approaching, and women I met were either seeing someone or had steady boyfriends already. Girls in my church were already paired off, getting married or just not interested in me. I was starting to question myself. Maybe God doesn't want me to have a soul mate. But, until God told me to stop looking, I wasn't going to stop.

Then it occurred to me: I needed to be more specific in my prayer to God. I was asking for a soul mate and possible future wife. Then I realized I had never asked God for a *devoted woman of God*. It may sound strange, but I also asked for a soul mate that was an orphan; a lonely young lady that was out there by herself. Someone who was searching for a knight in shining armor to rescue her from all of her hurts. *I* could be that someone that could fill that missing love in her life. I promised God that I would give her all the love humanly possible, always remembering what a precious gift from God she would be to me. I even asked God for a specific hair color and height. One last thing I asked for in my ideal woman was a gentle spirit; a woman that just required love, so there would always be peace in our home.

Then, my most important test came: I met Beryl. I fell in

love with her at first sight. It seemed like all my salesman training on *how to read people's intentions* went out the window. I'll never forget a lesson 'taught' to me by my best friend's father. He said, "If you ever see a pretty girl and she is with a real ugly friend, first approach the ugly girlfriend, then you introduce yourself to the pretty one. Then they will both like you."

One night, there she was! In the middle of a dance floor was the woman of my dreams! The only problem was that she was surrounded by not one, but two of the ugliest girls I had ever seen. I was the only guy brave enough to approach them. Other guys that night weren't willing to take the chance, but I was. Well, there she was...mine for the taking. The two homely friends that I had to get her away from happened to be sisters.

It was apparent to me that Beryl wasn't a superficial person. She seemed to possess genuine love from the heart. God had given me His discernment. Without saying a word, I recognized a good moral and spiritual person in Beryl. There was something pure and special about her. Even though we had just met, she told me her life story. It was like we already knew each other. I listened intently, not wanting to miss a single word.

When Beryl and I started dating, I sensed there was a distrust of men in general. I couldn't understand why this stunning blonde wasn't married or seeing anyone at the age of 28. When I first saw Beryl, I didn't mean to stare, but I was, and I couldn't keep my eyes from looking her direction. I couldn't help noticing, in a moment of time, that a mutual attraction was now between us. It was a magnet drawing us together. Trying to suppress emotions was really hard, and I didn't want to be tricked by love itself. But, inside I felt like I was going to burst. Was this the partner I'd been searching for? It was like everyone in the room had disappeared; there was no turning back now. She made me feel like some kind of superman that just came into her life.

I was committed in getting to know her. It was obvious after we started talking there was something uniquely different about how she valued life. Every person she discussed had a special quality about them. Beryl made everyone she met feel so important. She had a respect and redeeming admiration for people.

After spending hours talking to each other, it felt like only a few minutes had passed. I didn't want the night to end. I wondered and hoped if there would be a tomorrow for us. I couldn't help but think about that Four Seasons song, *'Tonight you're mine...but will you still love me tomorrow?'* My passion was now making the decisions which my head should. Wishing I hadn't revealed so much of my dreams for the future, there was a sense of uncertainty between us. Throwing caution to the wind, we both could be setting ourselves up for a heart break, but that was a risk we both were willing to take.

All I could anticipate was the day we would share our first kiss. When Beryl handed me her phone number, I looked her right in the eyes and asked if this was really her number? She apologized to me and wrote the real one down. Obviously, I wasn't about to let this opportunity of a lifetime pass me by. This could be the girl of my dreams. To me, that was proof that there was no man in her life and that was fine by me. I received it as a sign that God was saving her for me. After the night had ended, it felt like a dream. Was it real? Or just a figment of my imagination? After getting up the next morning, I checked my wallet to make sure I did have her phone number. It wasn't a dream. Hallelujah!

Every fiber in my body was telling me she's the one. Loneliness was about to lose a couple of old friends. In an unsuspecting moment, two lonely people were about to fall in love and become inseparable.

Now I was determined not to be included in the mix of rejected men. There was going to be a definitive outcome. My mission was clear to me. There would be a determined effort to not only capture her heart, but win her confidence and sweep her off her feet.

Our first date had finally arrived, and I was rehearsing in my head what I would say or not say. I realized that the last time we spoke, I was probably too transparent and hoping I didn't come across as too aggressive, so I needed to curb my excitement. I kept wondering what she thought of me. What happened next surprised the heck out of me. We went to a small cafe. It was a very intimate setting. The conversation got started, and continued where we left off a week ago. Beryl had become so at ease with me, she informed me that if a ring wasn't on her finger within a years' time, I would be history! Wow, this might be moving too fast for *me*.

I give her credit for being so honest. She told me later in the relationship that she thought I wasn't the type of guy to make a commitment. I responded with, "don't you think that question was a bit pushy?" Her response was, "I didn't want you wasting my time if you weren't serious." Was she pledging her love, or just testing me? I was delighted with all this undeserving, intense affection. The love and attention felt good. I've always been a true romantic and wanted to enjoy the courtship. I wanted to savor every moment we spent together. We knew we had opposite personalities. Beryl is a soft-spoken, sweet, feminine, affectionate lady; very kind and polite. On the other hand, I tend to be aggressive, and a take-charge person.

But this *man of God* was different than anyone she had met before. Because of Beryl's previous hurts, my unconditional love would be the remedy for healing her wounded heart. I needed to convince Beryl that my passion for her was now turning into pure love. One necessary detail which sealed the deal for me was that we shared the same faith in God. Without that, the relationship would be in vain.

I knew patience would be key in this relationship, and it eventually paid off. I became the number one man in her life, and we were going to be married.

It was the best decision I ever made. A lifetime of happiness was before me.

Beryl grew up in a home with mostly sisters and one younger brother, who suffered a handicap. The only strong male figure in Beryl's life was her father, whom she loved very much. Sadly, Beryl's Father passed away when she was thirteen years old. After hearing this, I discovered a void was left in Beryl's heart for a long time. She had no father figure to look after her. As if things weren't bad enough, Beryl's mother Margaret remarried Bob, a recovering alcoholic. Bob was considered a dry drunk. He appeared to be a sweet, old gentleman until about two weeks before their marriage, when his true colors came out. He became verbally abusive. Because of his unbearable behavior, Beryl had to move out.

Whatever obstacles we faced, the fact of the matter was, Beryl and I were in love and nothing would stop us from marrying.

Because of our age, we started a family right away. Our first born was a son. We named him Nicholas. He was a third generation Nicholas. We were ecstatic. I couldn't wait for him to grow up. There was so much I wanted to teach my son. Everything my father taught me plus everything I had experienced.

When Beryl was pregnant with our second child, it was supposed to be another boy, according to my Albanian grandmother, Mary Rado. Grandmother was always correct in her predictions. Well, not this time.

This sent us into a frenzy. No one had given a baby shower for my wife, so after we prepared for a boy we had to think quickly. One responsibility placed on me was choosing a name for my daughter. Beryl had a difficult childbirth and was in no condition to help me. I was thinking about my wife's name Beryl, which is found in the last book of the Bible.

In the scripture right next to Beryl, we found the seventh stone called *Chrysolyte,* from which I derived the name Crystal, a special gem from Heaven. It was a great way to honor God, and would be a shining reflection of her mother. Both my girls had names from the Bible.

I was determined to raise Crystal without the difficulties my wife had to endure in her life. We wanted her to be fearless, with no insecurities. In case something happened to me, I wanted to prepare Crystal to be able to handle herself in the real world, wanting her to be a leader in life.

We had great plans for Crystal, but sometimes when looking back, I realized I was too anxious to see her grow up. Because she was a girl, we were very protective of her. She was born with a speech impediment that would get her so frustrated when trying to communicate with us. It was heartbreaking to see. You could tell she understood every word spoken, but could not effectively respond.

When first hearing the diagnosis, we were devastated. My spirit wasn't going to accept it, especially when a God in Heaven knows me by name. Besides, I knew another doctor in Heaven called the Great Physician. So, we called on Him in prayer. In less than a year, Crystal spoke beautifully. She learned to first speak through her eyes. She also taught herself to thoroughly think things through before choosing her words. Because of this, her handicap became a honed tool that God could use.

This challenge built a determination and drive that molded Crystal's character. She had been delayed in developing. She needed to catch up. Her demeanor had become extremely motivated and focused for life itself. She would have to work harder that any of her peers, just to stay equal. Crystal wasn't content with the status quo. She was very competitive, and a sore loser at that. As parents, we would always encourage her with this Bible verse: Philippians 4:13 *"I can do all things through Christ which strengthens me."* With God *for* Crystal, who could be against her?

What we first viewed as a curse was now a blessing. One of Crystal's first phrases spoken was "Me do it." At a young age, she was very focused in accomplishing any-thing she started. Her character was being formed. Later in life she also was trained to carefully proceed before she committed to any-thing. Crystal chose to converse with a few people in her life that she felt comfortable with. There were some who viewed her as shy and others who were cynical, that viewed her as stuck up, but she was neither. She would listen carefully and choose her words.

At five years old, we noticed Crystal's life was starting to dramatically change. She made a conscious decision early in life that she would rather live as a lion than a thousand years as a lamb. Fear would have no place in her heart. Later on in life, she would prove this to many. When Crystal was three years old, we took her for swimming lessons, because we were going on vacation to Florida, and her aunt Kathy had a swimming pool. Crystal discovered she loved to swim. I remember taking her to the pool at the Disney resort. As we passed the 12-foot section marker, Crystal broke free from my hand and jumped right in! I panicked but, not wanting to alarm or frighten her, I hid my astonishment that she was swimming in 12 feet of water like it was nothing. Where did she get all this courage from? I am just glad my wife didn't witness that.

Crystal's older brother Nicholas was a very friendly and giving child. But, he started having problems in the neighborhood. Kids were jealous of Nick because his family owned their own home and most families on our street were renters. Kids can sure be mean. Older kids were stealing and breaking his stuff. Then the bullying started. Not wanting this to affect his sweet personality, we knew something had to be done. It was time to start training him in the Martial Arts. His childhood was over; innocence was about to be turned into maturity. At first, my wife was against this, but I was convinced it was the right thing to do.

I knew a three-time World Karate Champion from Okinawa, Japan. Master Teruyuki Higa. We told him the situation with Nicholas. He assured us if Nicholas was willing to train hard, we would see some results in a few months. Master Higa ran a no-nonsense karate school. It was considered to be brutal and used 'Old World' training methods. Master Higa had no sympathy for the weak or the fearful. Oftentimes, the training would produce pain. Master Higa would accept students as young as five years old. Their training would consist of full-contact fighting, to the face, as well as the body area. Protective gear was used, as well as training with weapons such as knives and throwing stars.

Most people drop out after a while because it is just too brutal for them. Before we started, I prepared Nicholas for what he would be facing. After studying under Master Higa myself for many years, I knew what challenges Nicholas would endure. On a warm July afternoon we began the road work; a two and a half mile run. Nicholas was ten years old and fairly athletic. I thought he should be able to handle that. As we were about to start from the house, Crystal, barely five years old, wanted to go with us. It was hard to leave her behind. I had to tell her "No," she was too young. We told her to stay with Mom and we would be right back.

After returning, my wife came out of the house asking, "Where's Crystal?" We said, "She's in the backyard where we left her." Panic struck in our hearts as we started frantically looking for her. I remember spotting her in the distance running up the block. She ran the same path we did. We couldn't believe our eyes. The majority of parents might have been upset or angry, but not us. We saw courage displayed in our daughter. Crystal wanted to show us that she was able to accomplish anything that came her way.

Most parents might have punished her because she disobeyed, but we weren't like most parents. Crystal wanted to be a part of the family. She was willing to participate in anything required of her no matter what the challenges were. Completely dehydrated and drenched in sweat, the only thing that was driving her was her determined will. That day we recognized a champion.

Part of Nicholas' training routine was duct-taping light bar bells to his hands and leg weights while running. He was required to keep this up at all times. Well guess who wanted to undergo the same? You guessed it! We taped flashlight batteries to Crystal's hands and smaller weights to her legs. I would make them run up and down the bleachers. After a couple of months of training, we were ready to join the karate school.

We had to promise Crystal that anytime Nicholas and I trained, she would come with us. When we signed Nicholas up for karate lessons, I didn't want Crystal to come, but she insisted on joining too. I was going to need a few karate lessons myself, because when my wife found out I signed Crystal up she was going to kill me!

MEMBERSHIP CARD

This is to Certify that
CRYSTAL SKULA

is a registered member of the
Okinawa Kenpo Karate - Do
Association
U. S. Headquarters
HOLDING THE RANK OF
2ND JR. YELLOW
Degree   Belt

Membership No. 3114

Date Issued 2/28/98

MASTER TERUYUKI HIGA
U. S. REPRESENTATIVE
7 TH DEGREE BLACK BELT

It wasn't long before Crystal started to excel. Whatever she learned in class was practiced at home. For over five years, brother and sister took karate lessons three times a week. Crystal participated in many demonstrations and countless fighting sessions. She was now living in a man's world, confident and self-assured. I often wondered if this was right for her; being a female and Dad having so much influence in her life.

The one time I considered pulling Crystal out of the karate school was when her first full contact fight was going to take place. The teacher announced this was his only female fighter in the class and Sensei Higa said, "Don't under-estimate her!" As they were gearing up for battle, chest protectors were put in place, as well as head gear. The boxing gloves were on and foot protectors adjusted. Before they engaged, Master Higa verbally instructed Crystal to show no mercy to her male opponent. He asked her if she knew what the meaning of no mercy meant?

She replied, "No."

At the age of five, she had never been posed a question like that before. He told Crystal if she kills her opponent during the fight, don't worry about it! That's what "no mercy" means. I really wasn't too comfortable with him saying that statement.

As the moment arrived, butterflies filled my stomach. I was concerned for my daughter's safety. Her face might get bruised! I've seen a kid lose his tooth during a fight. I remember asking Crystal that morning if she really wanted to go through with this and that I wouldn't mind if she canceled. (Matter of fact, I was hoping she would say yes, but that just wasn't my daughter.) Crystal insisted on going. She really wanted to overcome this new challenge she faced. She trained so hard for this day. Not knowing who her opponent would be, she was determined there was going to be only one winner and it was going to be her. I tried to tell her, "You can't predict the outcome of a fight," but no matter what the outcome, her opponent was in the fight of his life.

As Crystal squared off with her opponent, she was waiting to hear the Japanese word *Hajime* which means to begin fighting. It seemed like it took forever, but in a deep, loud voice Master Higa yelled it out. After hearing the command, it broke the tension and the fight was on. It started as an even match but soon Crystal was dominating the fight. Fear apparently gripped her opponent's heart. Crystal wasn't about to back off. As everyone started cheering for her, the nervous feeling we'd had earlier turned to pure excitement. She was about to experience her first taste of real victory; a champion trapped inside a quiet, shy five year old whose spirit spoke louder than any words she could ever say.

There was no question a new force was present; an unexpected, emerging female fighter had arrived. Master Higa was extremely pleased. He commented on what he called Crystal's fighting spirit. God gave her that spirit of boldness. God was training her for a greater purpose later in her life.

Now our little girl was motivated more than ever. She had become obsessed with being the best. Crystal rose to a new standard of excellence. She always pushed herself beyond the edge of the challenge. She was self-motivated, never needing any encouragement in accomplishing her dreams. Crystal never forgot that day's lesson. She always applied her hard work ethic and dedication in everything she faced. She made me so proud!

2

THY FAITHFULNESS

"Who then is a faithful and wise servant, whom his lord hath made ruler over his household, to give them meat in due season?" –Matthew 24:45

One thing that can be said about our family is that we always strive to be faithful to God in all things. This life we've chosen to live has been, at times, hard. We have viewed pleasing God as the reason we exist, with bumps and twists along the way. But, no matter what has come our way, the Lord has always made sure we knew that He was with us. We have never lost our joy for the things of God.

When Nicholas and Crystal were small, we didn't want them to miss out on the experience of a traditional church family upbringing. There came a time in my life when I was working two full-time jobs, one for our income and one for the church. My priorities were all wrong. I knew the order: God should be first in our life, then our family, then Christian service. Many great men and women of God have made this mistake in priority and paid a price for it. Having things in the wrong order could and has turned families away from the things of God. So we took a short leave and joined a smaller, local neighborhood church.

In the past, we had been involved in outreach ministry and

start-up works. I wanted my children to be schooled and trained in a background similar to the way their mother and I grew up, so we took a temporary leave from street ministry. We appreciated the people from the new church that took an immediate interest in us and encouraged our young children in the Lord.

For a while, we were content enjoying the sweet fellowship, soaking in the Word of God, and basking in biblical knowledge. My new ministry commitment was helping collect the offering and occasionally teaching a Bible class.

But we recall a time, before our children were born, when the Lord first called us to ministry. It all started like a whirlwind. We had no real experience, nor did we know what to expect or whether we would have any help. But in my spirit a new season was about to begin. There was no audible voice, but a desire in my soul that I didn't yet recognize. There was definitely a change in the winds blowing through our lives. We were sensing something was about to occur; our life course was about to change. We had expectations, but couldn't see anything just yet. We would have to accept whatever came our way by faith.

Jim and Joan Thornton reached out to us and took us under their wings. The Thornton's taught us the importance of faithfulness in serving God. After working with them for a short while, they were called to a new work in Arizona. When they left, they felt led to entrust us with their children's ministry, which they had built and served over twenty years, called AWANA. AWANA is a two-hour program, every Friday night that includes a Bible memory contest, counsel time and sports. The word AWANA is taken from the Bible verse in *2nd Timothy 2:15* "*Study to shew thyself approved unto God, a workman that needeth not to be ashamed, rightly dividing the word of truth.*"

We had been fairly new to the church and had been chosen over many faithful leaders and workers who had been there since the beginning. Even though we didn't fully understand their decision, we accepted it by faith as divine favor from God. Immediately after the Thornton's left, there was a change of attitude among our coworkers. Some thought we were not up to the challenge and perhaps too green for the task. Some were likely offended because we were chosen over them. Others tried to discourage us by complaining and murmuring. We were determined to endure whatever God's calling was to be in our lives, no matter what the cost. We believed that whatever the popular opinion was, despite my inexperience, God would equip and mold us for His greater purpose. Even though there were whispers of negativity and fear that we were going to ruin the ministry, it was the Word of God and pure obedience that got us through this testing of our faith.

Unfortunately, we got our first lesson in church politics. No matter how great the church, there can always be wolves among us. We were *reminded* about how things had been working for years and that if we wanted to be successful, we should follow the footsteps of our predecessors. After many nights of praying, it was revealed to me that I needed to know who my friends were and who were not. We imposed a new standard that would set apart the people that were really listening to the heart of God. Ministry leaders would have to be active soul winners as well as prayer warriors. They would have to bear the burdens of the children's lives they were called to serve. God had entrusted them to our care. Clearly, there are times when it's better to work with a few dedicated Christians than many 'Sunday morning' helpers.

If we were going to expect great things from God, He needed to see that we were diligent in seeking Him. Most of the complainers dropped out, but the faithful ones stayed and saw great and mighty works of God come to pass. It was almost funny to see the people who didn't want to share the new vision all of a sudden have a change of heart. When things started changing for the better, everyone wanted to be a part of the ministry.

The children's outreach averaged about sixty neighborhood kids on Friday nights, but the majority of them still didn't come to Sunday services. As the church established a bus ministry with one van, the children's youth group really took off, and we eventually added two big school buses. At one point, we were experiencing bigger crowds at the church on Fridays than at Sunday's services. (*Then the pastor reminded me that you can't build a church around children.*)

But, excitement filled the air on Friday nights. No matter how tired we were, the minute we touched the church door we could feel the energy charge our spirits. And when each meeting ended, no one ever wanted to leave. Some would linger around for hours just sharing what God was showing them. It was one of those mountaintop experiences that comes around once in a life time; a special time as a family that we will never forget.

With this influx of new children, we seized the opportunity to visit the parents and share the Gospel of Jesus Christ. Before long, the newly saved parents were becoming leaders in the church. One day the pastor came to me and asked for a vision for the upcoming year. I replied, "I would like to see the ministry double to 400 children." After publishing this in the church bulletin, one of my leaders came to me upset, complaining about the logistic nightmare it would cause, and suggested I pick a smaller number. After all, where would we put all these new children?' I told her to let God worry about that. Then the children started to share their faith with their peers and bring their friends to youth group.

Many unexplained blessings occurred during this time. My company bought an old cookie truck, sight unseen. When we looked inside, it was filled with fresh cookies. We called the cookie company and they said to keep them, that it was part of the deal. After giving everyone I knew a box of cookies, we still had an enormous amount left. That Friday night after the meeting, we told the kids we had a special surprise for them...cookies for all! The kids went wild.

About a dozen teenage girls visited the youth meeting one night. Even though they had a good time and were planning to come back soon, they did not respond to the Gospel message. At that time, there was a famous Christian radio teacher, who was broadcasting that the *Second Return of Christ* would come tonight! They all started thinking back to their decision not to receive Christ when they were given the invitation the previous Friday night. But, upon hearing those words; *"that if you were found without Christ during the Rapture, you would be left behind,"* they panicked!

After the broadcast, they frantically called the church, only to find there was no one answering the phone. Fear struck their hearts, and they believed the Rapture had already occurred and they were left behind, so they were desperately trying to find out for sure. They anxiously ran three miles to the church to find some answers. By the time they all got there, the girls were hysterically crying, believing they had missed their chance to receive Christ and have eternal life. They were a bunch of sorrowful, lost souls looking into an empty church, banging on the doors, feeling desperate and disappointed. If only they could have a second chance, their decision would be *yes* this time.

God answers prayers. The pastor surprisingly opened the church doors to see what the commotion was all about. These hysterical young girls rushed to the pastor, all talking at the same time. After calming them down, he assured them the Rapture hadn't taken place yet and he would be more than willing to lead them to the Lord in prayer. That day all twelve girls received Jesus as their personal Savior. That afternoon I received a call from the pastor and still remember the excitement in his voice!

At the next Friday AWANA meeting, the altar was full of young people, giving their hearts to the Lord. The pastor and I have shared a good laugh about that from time to time and thank God for that *phony radio preacher* that day.

"But of that day and hour knoweth no man, no, not the angels of heaven, but my Father only." (Matthew 24:36)

Years have passed and we lost contact with the girls. I wonder if they think back to their salvation decision that afternoon, and the experience that led up to it. I pray that they are all serving God today.

After many, many times of testing of our faith, I was hoping God would give us a rest. But instead, God was grooming us for the test of our lives. As the leader of the ministry, it was important to lead by example. When a new kid would sign up to join the group, we made a point of visiting the home and explaining what the ministry was about. It gave us the opportunity to invite the entire family to visit our church.

There was one follow-up visit that we will never forget. We had an odd number of 'soul winners' one night, and we usually try to pair women with women and men with men. Because there was no one for me to pair up with, I went out that night with two sisters from the church. The family we visited was a single mother of two: a teenage daughter who attended the AWANA clubs and a younger boy that seemed to have some kind of disability.

Their apartment building was located in Bay Shore, New York. It was a drug-ridden neighborhood. Usually visits from the church were well received. The local drug dealers and thugs didn't bother us as they knew who we were.

The church also ran a food pantry and distributed donations to the neighborhood from the church van. But that cold winter night, we were all in for a shocking surprise. After knocking on the door, we were greeted with a barrage of profanities. An evil force was resisting our presence there. We could tell something greater than the lady's anger was fueling the fire.

My two companions were astonished by how we were

greeted. They started praying for this lady as I tried speaking to her. Even though it seemed in vain, the prayer partners didn't stop praying as I was presenting the Gospel. But, this mother was convinced we were trying to brainwash her daughter into joining some kind of cult.

All of a sudden something changed in the conversation! The mother's heart was starting to soften. It was unbearably cold in the hallway, and we wanted to step into her foyer where it was warmer. Before we got a chance to ask permission, a wave of heat consumed us. A minute ago everyone was shivering, and less than a moment later we were all starting to sweat! A calmness came over us all, and before we knew it, the girl's mother was repeating the Lord's Prayer and receiving Christ as her Savior. Immediately after praying, a transformed person was standing before us!

Her angry demeanor was now turned to joy. I asked one of the sisters afterward if they noticed the sudden burst of heat that filled the hallway. They had also felt the presence of the Holy Ghost, and knew there was a spiritual struggle taking place, and God would be the Victor! I was ecstatic after that happened. I never experienced God's power like that before. I was shocked that God even considered using me. It was a once-in-a-lifetime experience in and of itself. I wanted to shout from the rooftops what God allowed us to see that night, but I was afraid no one would believe what had happened...*Nor could we ever really explain it.*

3

DISPLAYS OF MEEKNESS

"Put on therefore, as the elect of God, holy and beloved, bowels of mercies, kindness, humbleness of mind, meekness, longsuffering" –Colossians 3:12

Meekness is a word that is often confused or believed to be associated with the word *weakness*. The actual meaning of the word weakness is a state of being powerless, lacking any strength or power to sustain one's self. Weakness is a terrible, hopeless feeling, causing a person to be desperate to draw strength, to restore their life.

Meekness is often found in Christians that occupy a reserved, hidden strength in their spirit. It is a peace that comes from God, with a confidence in knowing God controls all things. Christians possess a great power that is totally under the influence or the direction of the Holy Spirit. It is a great virtue and a "must" to have in the Christian life. A great illustration of this is the magnificent thoroughbred race horse, sleek and powerful, allowing itself to be pet by strangers, but solely under the control of his handlers. It appears to the natural eye and touch as a gentle and docile animal, until the command is given and a transformation takes place before one's eyes. This once quiet thoroughbred transforms itself and unleashes a fiery force of stamina that displays an impressive, graceful show of speed.

The best example of meekness in human form can be found in the Bible. A prophecy from the book of Isaiah, (Isaiah 9:6-7) states that God's only begotten Son would be born in the family line of King David. He would be called Mighty God, Everlasting Father, and Prince of Peace. When Jesus arrived, He took the form of human flesh. The believers of that day were expecting a God of fire that would rule by force. The disciples realized the power of a mighty God was contained in Jesus' human body, but didn't fully understand the true purpose of God's will.

Jesus needed to live a perfect, sinless life in human form. Jesus set an example for all Christians to follow. Many times Jesus displayed the mighty power of God by performing miracles such as walking on water, calming the winds and the sea, casting out demons, and raising the dead. Jesus never abused His power and lived a peaceful life, pleasing to His Heavenly Father. This was all taking place while living under a repressive, occupying Roman government with an abusive army. Believers of God wanted God's kingdom to rule the world and take Israel's enemies by force. God's ways are not man's ways. God knew man needed a New Covenant.

No one ever expected God to dwell among us in human form. His Spirit is now sealed with us and we are united with God forever. As Christians, we possess a dual citizenship; Heaven is our new awaited home. Under God's control, a Spirit-filled Christian denies his self-interests and puts God first. So, a familiar mark of a Christian is a spirit of meekness, which waits on God for an answer. It's not easy to do when we're in the flesh. God only works through the Spirit.

After learning about the virtue of meekness, I wanted my children to possess this characteristic in their lives. Possessing meekness in your character can protect you from pride, ego, and conceit, and keep a person humble, down to earth, and real. Whoever thought physically fit, aggressive people, or weak, soft-spoken people – wealthy or poor – could both possess this virtue.

One example that surprised me was found in my daughter Crystal. When you, as a parent, believe in some kind of virtue or morals, without saying a word, your children will emulate your actions. Even if a young person doesn't fully understand the virtue, they learn it from their parents by watching them move under the direction of the Holy Spirit.

One day, a new family moved into our neighborhood down the block. School was out and it was early summer. We never got an opportunity to introduce ourselves. They had two little girls Crystal's age. Their mother spotted Crystal playing in the yard while driving down the block. The girl's mother sent them over to introduce themselves to Crystal. When my wife answered the door, these girls asked if a little girl lived here and if they could meet her. We were happy because, at the time, Crystal had no one her age to play with. They all became fast, close friends. The Shaw family was renting a big old house down the block that had been empty for some time. The neighbors were glad to see it occupied.

By the time we took notice, the family was gutting the interior, redoing everything, from the ceilings to new roof, new cement sidewalks, and driveways. They even installed a swimming pool with a wrap-around deck. When their kitchen was complete, it was a state of the art design. The oven was stainless steel. It looked like it belonged in a professional restaurant. When large screen televisions first came out, the Shaw family had the biggest one I had ever seen.

But what struck me as strange was all the money that was poured into this rental. It was something a homeowner would do; definitely not a renter. This all happened in a matter of a few weeks.

When Crystal found out they had purchased a new pool, she was excited. She loved to swim. Crystal would swim from sun up to sun down if we would let her. Crystal was treated as their other daughter. The family couldn't get enough of Crystal. The friends would play together day and night. We felt she was safe there. Mr. Shaw had arranged an open tab with the ice cream truck. Whenever the truck stopped in front of their house, anybody that wanted ice cream got it. Word spread quickly throughout the neighborhood. Now when the truck pulled up, there was a mob of kids waiting.

Another, troublesome neighbor had gotten into a jam with a South American drug gang and his life was in danger. He had three sons; two of them were disabled young boys in wheelchairs. He was the sole breadwinner of the family. His problem was addiction: he was a crack-head. He had just ripped off this gang's drugs. The gang was coming to his house for one of two outcomes; either to collect the money (which he didn't have) for drugs that were gone or to make an example out of him. There was nowhere to hide. He had to face them.

In a desperate attempt to save his own hide, he sent his son – the one son without a disability – to reach out to the neighborhood for help. This young man was in tears and begged every neighbor to help his father. I cautiously looked on from a distance. I didn't need to get caught up in the middle of something that was none of my business, although I wasn't about to let anything bad happen to the family. Calling the police wasn't an option. It might make matters worse. If enough support could be raised, the problem could be resolved, I reasoned. Because there was great sympathy for the family, the entire block showed up, with bats, chains, and even a pitch fork. It was starting to look like a horror movie.

When two car loads of South American gang members showed up, the neighbors were ready to give them a "warm welcome," but within minutes, Mr. Shaw played a role in solving the problem. I was told he had some of his *associates* advise the gang to forget about what they were thinking of doing, and believe it or not, we never saw or heard from them again.

It was like the Shaw family had become heroes overnight and the neighborhood was taken by storm. We couldn't believe the next thing we heard; Mr. Shaw was asked to be the assistant high school football coach, after only living in the neighborhood a couple of months.

One day, a football player had to be cut from the team. The boy's father was outraged and blamed Mr. Shaw for the decision. This father was determined to do something about the situation. The family happened to live down the block from the Shaw family. Not long after, the boy's parents drove past the Shaw home, and spotted him coming out of his house with their baby sitter. They slammed the brakes on and their car came to a screeching halt. The doors flew open and they rushed out and proceeded to beat up Mr. Shaw *and* the babysitter. In a matter of seconds the two had to be hospitalized. The police showed up too late to help, but arrested the football player's parents. The community became outraged when finding out about the incident. Mr. Shaw received an outpouring of sympathy. As a thank you gesture, he threw an open block party at his house.

When I received an invitation through Crystal, I declined the offer and decided to draw back and keep my distance. Strange as it seemed, a couple days before the party, there was a knock at my front door. Mr. Shaw was at my door in person. He was worried I was offended by the way the invitation was presented to me. I thanked him for his concern toward me and said, maybe next time. Mr. Shaw had a charismatic personality. He was very persuasive. He could have been a mayor. But after the incident involving that gang, I felt I should keep some distance between us. Crystal was begging me to go, and so was Mr. Shaw, so I agreed to go for a little while, just to please Crystal.

When I first got there, I couldn't believe my eyes. There was lobster, fillet mignon, steak, and lots of shrimp. They had an outside bar and even the ice cream truck was parked there to supply ice cream for the kids. There were two live bands playing. The fireworks display was nothing short of spectacular. There was face painting for the children and even pony rides. It was extravagant.

The question that everyone wanted to ask him was, "Where does all this money come from?" He was a renter and said he had no intentions of buying and yet he spent thousands of dollars in this middle class neighborhood. Now he's lending money to everyone that needs it, too? Whenever he would order pizza, it was ten pizzas at a time, to give the rest to the neighbors. The generosity of the Shaw's was incredible. They owned several ATVs, mini bikes, and go-karts and let the neighborhood kids use them any time they wanted to.

One day after work, I was about a block away from my home when I noticed the police were staked out at the end of the street. Suddenly, I saw Mr. Shaw riding his ATV recklessly, at a high rate of speed down the block, with the police right behind him. As the police attempted to cut him off, in an effort to stop him, he avoided them and cut through the sidewalks across someone's lawn. After dodging and evading the police, the crazy fool turned back and tried to provoke another police chase. His good luck had ended.

They finally got him.

After seeing this, I thought he was out of his mind, and was going to be arrested and put in jail. He must of have had the luck of the Irish. I couldn't believe it! His only consequences were traffic tickets and getting his ATV impounded. He walked away Scot-free. What disturbed me about Mr. Shaw was his demeanor. He was calm, and he wasn't concerned *at all* about losing the ATV or receiving the many tickets. The very next day, at the same time, in the same place, Mr. Shaw was now riding a brand new ATV, doing *the same* foolish routine as the day before. I summoned him to stop, wanting to know what had happened the day before. He told me the police had impounded the ATV and issued tickets. When I asked him if he was going to bail his ATV out of the impound lot, he told me he didn't like that old ATV anyway, and it was easier to just buy a new one. I still couldn't understand his logic.

The only thing Mr. Shaw didn't share with anyone was his 1957 Chevy Bel Air in mint condition, which he kept in the garage at all times...that and his secret life. Eventually the truth always comes out. Mr. Shaw had a secret profession: bank robber. We had a real live gangster living among us. Deep in everyone's heart, we all sensed something was awry. He must have been very successful, somehow, we thought; he sure lived "high on the hog."

After being arrested and with his face in the newspaper, people couldn't believe it. This great family man and good neighbor was nothing but a two-bit crook. I felt sick about allowing my daughter to be exposed to all of this. I was told later his family had no idea what he was involved in. Suddenly, the fast friends and neighbors started distancing themselves from the family, despite all the fun times and good things he did. He was now characterized as a no-good crook.

My daughter was devastated by the news. She would only see the good side of people. Crystal was a loyal person and stood by her two friends. She was seven years old, but just her presence there was a comfort to them during their darkest hour.

Kids can really be mean. One day a group of kids came by the Shaw house to let the girls know just what a crook their father was, and that they should be ashamed of what their Dad did. This was too much for a couple of little girls to emotionally handle. Both the sisters broke down in tears, crying uncontrollably. Something great rose up inside of

Crystal, which might be the greatest moment in her friends' lives to endear them to her. Little Crystal jumped into the middle of the crowd in defense of her friends and told them, *"Don't worry about a thing; JESUS WILL FORGIVE YOUR FATHER!"*

Everyone was now silent because quiet, shy little Crystal had the courage to speak God's truth in the middle of opposition. I remember hearing this for the first time from a neighbor. My soul soared and we were so proud of what God was doing in her life at such a young age. Crystal, whether she knew it or not, had displayed an act of *meekness with courage*! We thanked God for making Crystal a mixture of beauty, strength and grace in the form of a little girl.

As the summer came to an end, so did the relationship with the Shaw family. We would never see them again. I hoped Crystal touched their lives, and the seeds she planted from God would grow in their hearts. The last we heard, Mr. Shaw was sentenced to fifteen years in prison. The rest of the family moved to Connecticut with their grandmother. As we pass the house where they used to live, it's sad to see it all run down again. It was a flash of time in Crystal's life, but a story that would be talked about for a long time. It was quite an amazing experience for our little girl.

My Parents

Crystal
10/2/04

My parents are my roles models. They help me with my problems, always there for me and always taking care of me.

My Parents put me in God's path. They always bring me to church, even when it's snowing. My parents also bring me to Awana. Awana is a christian club for boys and Girls. We have game time, a fun lesson, and they have a book full of verses. The most verses I said in one night was 19 verses.

My Parents disclpline me when I am wrong. My dad alway tell me that he punish me because he love me so I will learn not to do it again.

Thank you!

4

CRYSTAL'S FRIENDS

"Greater love hath no man than this, that a man lay down his life for his friends." –John 15:13

Crystal's older brother, Nicholas, was her only sibling. He was a good friend, and she truly loved him with all her heart. Even though Crystal was four years younger, she often felt it necessary to protect *him*, believe it or not! When they were younger, they used to squabble, as most siblings do. But as they matured, there was a closeness between them that age, time and even death could not part.

One day, when Nicholas was about ten years old and Crystal was six, a neighborhood kid started a fight with him. Just as they were squaring off, Crystal jumped between them. Standing on her tippy toes, she yelled, "Don't you hurt my brother!" After hearing this story from people in the neighborhood, Crystal gained a lot of respect at an early age.

Crystal disliked bullies and wasn't afraid to confront them. Her sweet, quiet voice would speak out boldly against them, especially if she was defending her friends. One thing we could never understand about Crystal was that she never felt it necessary to defend *herself*. She just seemed to ignore situations aimed at her. I guess no one could really figure out what made her tick. One thing is for sure: she was not afraid. She wasn't a person outwardly full of emotion either. There was a calmness and a confidence in her spirit and a soul full of love.

Crystal made friends with a special young girl named Rebekah Chang. Rebekah was a beautiful young girl that had been born with Down Syndrome. Most young people Rebekah's age found it awkward to relate to her. Not knowing what a sweet, gentle soul Rebekah really was, it was their loss. As Crystal's parents, we were concerned at first about how the two would get along. Her disability didn't seem to bother Crystal, even though there was a four year age difference. Crystal was younger, but even though she had a higher mentality, it had no effect on the friendship.

Rebekah came from a diverse background. Her mother was a Jewish Christian, and her father was Chinese, born in Hong Kong. Because of the special needs of someone with Down Syndrome, people must understand that they are very loving individuals who respond to a little kindness and attention. Crystal sensed this need and offered it. Nicholas was tutored in math every Monday afternoon by Rebekah's mother, Mrs. Carin Chang. Rebekah always made sure her homework was done, as well as her chores, before Nicholas and Crystal came over. Mrs. Chang was a very gifted school teacher that poured her heart and soul not only into Rebekah, but the students she tutored, as well.

The time spent with Crystal was very precious to Rebekah. They would play board games, jump on the trampoline, and talk together. Rebekah prayed that Nicholas' tutoring would last forever, and I believed God answered Rebekah prayers. His tutoring lasted three years. As time moved on, Mrs. Chang went home to be with the Lord. With no mother to take care of Rebekah, the family had placed her in a group home for special needs kids. We often wonder if Rebekah still remembers her time spent with Crystal for those short years.

One of Crystal's dear friends from early childhood, Miss Megan Mohr, sent us a collection of definitions of friendship, which described her love for Crystal.

All friends are priceless.
A friend is one of the nicest things you can have,
and one of the best things you can be.
- Douglas Pagels

A true friend fills a place in your heart that
you never knew was empty.
-Unknown

If we are friends much longer, we'll start to look alike.
- Unknown

Friends are those rare people who ask how you are
and then wait for the answer.
- Unknown

A friend is somebody who has a close personal
relationship of mutual affection and trust with another.
The road to a friend's house is never long.
- Danish Proverb

Friends are family you choose for yourself.
A friend is a gift.
- Megan Mohr

There seems to be an emotional release when friends meet. They can put your spirit at ease. And in no time at all, you will be sharing your deepest secrets and find yourself laughing and forgetting the sorrow that previously held you from seeking your beloved friend.

Crystal's most magnificent gift was her attraction to little children. Everyone would call Crystal a kid magnet. Wherever kids were around they would seek her out, hoping to get close to her. They always wanted Crystal to play with them or just stay close to her side, even though they were much younger. Crystal was never without some kind of candy or gum. We weren't sure if that was to bribe kids to leave her alone or to please them! But one thing we knew was that she loved her little friends and always made time for them, making them feel very important.

There was a little boy that was on Crystal's school bus. The first day, he was nervous, being all alone for the first time coming to a new school. Crystal would talk to him and give him candy every morning on the way to school. Needless to say, they became good friends. Whenever Crystal was sick or not in school, her little friend would always ask for her. I guess Crystal was a source of comfort to the little boy. She would always give a friend her last piece of candy, or even money, if needed. Crystal's little cousins, Nicholas and Ashley, loved her so much, and she had a profound influence on them. They even named their new dog Crystal, after their favorite cousin.

Crystal was most attached to her mother, Beryl, who was her closest friend and loved one. Beryl was a stay-at-home mom. We both felt strongly about having Beryl be there for the children each day. It was a financial sacrifice, but it was worth it. Crystal would always tell her mother, "When I grow up, I want to be just like you."

My wife and Crystal worked as a team taking care of our home, and they always made it very nice. Our home was full of joy and love. Every holiday was an exciting time, especially Christmas. School would be closed for two weeks, and we were free to do whatever we wanted!

Beryl was a dedicated mother to both Crystal and Nicholas. Early on in their lives, Beryl devoted herself to a worldwide prayer group called *Mom's In Prayer International*. The prayer group was always held at the Smithtown Christian School where the kids attended. When Crystal and Nicholas would see their mother's car in the parking lot, it brought them both comfort. When they got home they wanted to know who was prayed for that day. You could only pray for one child at a time. No matter how much they would badger her, their mother would never tell them who she prayed for. She told them it was a secret. Beryl, along with the other mothers, would pray for them at least once a week for years.

Mothers are often their child's greatest prayer warrior. I was given this poem by Crystal and Nicholas' grandmother, Eleanor Skula:

THE WARRIOR
by Larry Clark

This morning my thoughts traveled along
To a place in my life where days have long since gone.
Beholding an image of what I used to be,
As visions were stirred, and God spoke to me.

He showed me a Warrior, a soldier in place
Positioned by Heaven, yet I saw not the face.
I watched as the Warrior fought enemies
That came from the darkness, with destruction for me.

I saw as the Warrior would dry away tears,
As all of Heaven's angels hovered so near.
I saw many wounds on the Warrior's face,
Yet weapons of warfare were firmly in place.

I felt my heart weeping, my eyes held so much,
As God let me feel, the Warrior's prayer touched.
I thought 'How familiar' the words that were prayed.
The prayers were like lightning that never would fade.

I said to God, "Please, the Warrior's name"
He gave no reply, He chose to refrain.

I asked, "Lord, who is broken that they need such prayer?"
He showed me an image of myself standing there.

Bound by confusion, lost and alone,
I felt prayers of the Warrior carry me home.
I asked, "Please show me, Lord, this warrior so true."
I watched and I wept, for Mother...it was you.

5

THE FAMILY PET

"And she said, Truth, Lord: yet the dogs eat of the crumbs which fall from their masters' table." –Matthew 15:27

Our family has a soft spot for animals. We started off with a goldfish named Buddy, who unfortunately, didn't survive long. One day at work, my co-workers and I heard a dog barking outside. It was going on for a while and it was starting to irritate us. My sister Nancy finally investigated. As she walked through a nearby wooded area, she found a little puppy tied to a tree, abandoned by some despicable person and who had left it there to die. After rescuing the puppy, the next question was what to do with this dog. We didn't want to take it to the pound, because if no one adopted it, I was afraid they might destroy it. So I took a chance, called my wife, and told her and the children that I had a big surprise for them when I got home that night.

They all took turns calling me at work, each trying to get me to spill the beans about the surprise. My lips were sealed. One speculation from my wife was that it was Chinese food. Another was a vacation, but no one's guess even came close. It was fun teasing them all and leaving them in suspense.

Finally, when my car pulled up to the front of the house, I noticed the front door was open in anticipation of my arrival. I had put the puppy in a cardboard box in an effort to keep it warm and hide it to prolong the excitement. As they watched me from the window, expecting me to walk toward the front door, I tricked them by running to the back door. By this time, they all ran to meet me at the back door and demanded to see what was in the box! I kept delaying and as the excitement kept building, they couldn't take it anymore. When they opened the box, all of them were in shock, especially my wife. They were *never* expecting to see a puppy.

Beryl's first reaction was, "Where's the Chinese food?" The kids were thrilled. They couldn't believe it! Though my wife's reaction wasn't as enthusiastic at first, I told her if she didn't like the dog we could bring it back. Her response was, "Yeah, right!" She wasn't about to say the dog had to go and be seen as the bad guy in this family. Crystal immediately decided to name the dog Rosie. We realized later that the name Rosie really matched her personality. When Rosie got excited, she would take off in the back yard, running in circles; first to the right and then to the left. Rosie was always jealous. She didn't like other dogs, cats, and *especially* not squirrels. If any animal dared to come into the yard – her sacred territory – Rosie would chase after them.

There was a lot of squabbling as to who our new pet belonged to. We told them she was everyone's dog, including the responsibilities for taking care of her. The competition began between Nicholas and Crystal to see who could win the most affection from Rosie. But things weren't so rosy at first. It soon became very apparent that this cute little puppy must have been abused and didn't trust people.

We didn't really get off to the best start with Rosie. A few times, she tried to bite me. Fortunately for me, I had been a dog trainer and saw it coming. A concern was raised about the safety for our children. Rosie was classified as a "fear biter." Rosie was behaving like a wild animal and had to be deprogrammed to adjust to living with kind people. The method that had to be used to train her was sometimes physical, but we took care not to break her spirit. It can be ugly to see, but the only alternative was to put the dog to sleep or send her back to the junk yard.

Not wanting to disappoint my children, they convinced me to try and save Rosie. It took some time, but Rosie eventually adjusted to her new family life, and we noticed she had become quite the character. Rosie loved Crystal's female friends and would follow them around the house. When they had to use our bathroom, the door didn't lock all the way and Rosie would open the bathroom door with her nose and walk in and join them. Of course, when we heard a scream, everyone started yelling, "Rosie!"

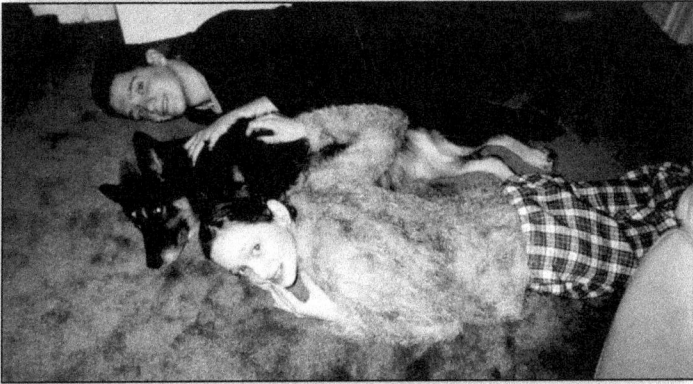

Time moved on swiftly, and when Crystal was a preteen, she discovered the book about the true life story of Ann Frank, a diary of a young girl hiding in Nazi Germany. Ann wrote about a family that had shown compassion on her and her family and hid them in their house, risking their own lives. They lived in constant fear of being discovered by the Nazis. Crystal was moved by the story and it left a lasting impression on her. She seemed to rediscover a new passion for people in need.

Right after reading the *Diary of Ann Frank*, a dramatic story broke on the news about a young girl taken from her home across the country in Utah. Constantly seeing this on the news greatly disturbed Crystal. The young girl's name was

Elizabeth Smart, and she was kidnapped right out of her bedroom window. The story was on the news for months. Crystal was Elizabeth's age and similar in appearance. Both had blond hair and fair complexions. Both girls had bedrooms upstairs. We followed the story unaware of how it might affect Crystal. We would pray during our family's daily devotions for Elizabeth's safe return to her family.

A side effect of Elizabeth's drama was revealed after Crystal's birthday party at a bowling alley. Since she loved to bowl, they gave her the gift of a real bowling pin. It was incredibly heavy. It struck me as a strange birthday gift for a young child, but Crystal thought it was great. My wife said she noticed Crystal was sleeping with that bowling pin by her pillow. I thought it was a bizarre item to choose to sleep with. Was it a hint she wanted us to take her bowling again? Finally the suspense was too much for me, so I asked, "What's the story with the bowling pin in your bed?"

She said, "Dad, if someone breaks into my room and tries to kidnap me, I am going to hit him over the head with the bowling pin."

I answered, "Good girl! That's a great idea!" and I left the room.

After thinking about it a minute, I added "If you ever get into a fight with your brother, please don't hit *him* with the bowling pin!"

She responded and said, "Yes Daddy."

As I walked away, I thought to myself proudly, *"That's my girl."*

In hindsight, we wondered if we should have shielded Crystal from that story. But, thankfully, she and Rosie had developed a beautiful bond between them. Rosie stayed with her at night calming all her fears. We were confident that

Rosie would protect Crystal at all costs. In my mind, Rosie had earned her place in the family. All our hearts went out to the Smart family. Many years later, we are grateful to God for reuniting their family once again.

6

CRYSTAL'S HUMOR LET THE GOOD TIMES ROLL!

"Then was our mouth filled with laughter, and our tongue with singing: then said they among the heathen, The Lord hath done great things for them." –Psalm 126:2

Crystal loved making people laugh. Sometimes she would mimic a person, playing their part with a humorous twist. She learned this routine from her brother. Often, mimes would perform at our public library. She and Nicholas would stand alongside the stage. Without being seen, they would copy the performance to a tee. The audience would break out in laughter. When the mime would turn to see what the crowd was laughing at, the kids maintained a straight face. It took some time for the mime to figure out what caused the laughs, but eventually Crystal and Nicholas would get discovered.

As a father, I had the unpleasant task of disciplining Crystal occasionally. This was a parenting duty I personally hated. One day, as a toddler, she threw a temper tantrum. She felt justified in her cause. The mistake she made was challenging my authority, so I spanked her and sent her to her room. When Beryl came home, I gave her an account of the day's events, including Crystal's misbehavior. Crystal, who was supposedly sleeping, had been listening to every word spoken. All of a sudden, we heard her yelling! "You people down-stairs better stop gossiping about me!" Beryl and I both started laughing hysterically. I think I laughed most of that night.

Crystal always emulated her Mom in everything she did. When she was two years old, we would put Crystal in our bedroom for naps and close the door so we could watch TV. One nap time, Crystal got up, pushed the door open and burst in wearing her mother's pantyhose, a set of high heels, and a pearl necklace. She posed like she was the cat's meow! We all cracked up laughing.

Nicholas and Crystal, always in competition with each other, once asked us, "Who's your favorite child?"

The answer was always the same, "Nicholas is my favorite son, and Crystal is my favorite daughter."

The next question was, "How much do you love me?"

The answer was the same. My wife would open her arms up as far as they would go and say, "This much."

Crystal would laugh and say, "That's all?"

Getting ready for school was a daily challenge for Nicholas. He wasn't as focused as Crystal. He would be getting dressed or shoving down breakfast as the bus was pulling away. Crystal took great delight in being the first one up in the morning, getting completely dressed and ready for school first. This is where the trouble started. She would tease Nicholas about his inability to get up and be dressed first. One morning, a bet was made to settle this argument once and for all. Crystal had gotten up extra early to show her brother that she was the true morning star. But that morning, she found him sleeping on the couch downstairs, covered in a blanket. As expected, as she started yelling in his ear that she won again, but Nicholas jumped up fully dressed and yelled, "I beat you, I beat you!"

Crystal, mad as a hornet, started screaming, "You cheated! You cheated!"

Another time, Nicholas wasn't happy about Crystal's organized manner, so he wanted to rattle her cage. So, on one Saturday morning, he ran into her room fully dressed in his school uniform and started shaking her awake from a dead sleep and screamed, "We overslept for school! Hurry and get dressed." She scurried about in a haze trying to get herself ready. When Crystal realized it was Saturday morning, she really went crazy! Nick got in trouble for that little stunt...

One afternoon, we went to get a prescription filled at the pharmacy. My wife decided it would be best if Nicholas, Crystal and I waited in the car while she ran in. We were all tired and welcomed the opportunity to rest. While waiting, we noticed a car pull in front of us with a mother, father and three children in their mid-teens. The mother was sitting in the car and looked extremely angry. We witnessed her screaming in the father's ear, as he was cowering away from her. Then she turned to her kids and started chastising them. We were hoping she was here at the pharmacy getting medicine for herself.

When the parents left the car to go inside, we could see the tension among the teens. We also observed that the car they were in was in mint shape; not a scratch on it, clean as whistle inside and out. Suddenly, out of nowhere, a great wind picked up and sent an empty shopping cart flying across the parking lot at breakneck speed. The shopping cart slammed into their car so hard it jolted the kids inside and put a huge dent in the side of the car.

When the kids realized what had happened, they started

laughing nervously, and so did we. When their parents came out and saw the car door caved in, no one was laughing. It was dead silence as we looked on. The mother had another meltdown and we decided she really had anger issues. We all agreed it wasn't proper to be laughing at her misery.

One night, one of Crystal's friends had permission from her mother to stay overnight. It was her friend Alana who was a beautiful girl, living a privileged life, in a large, beautiful home on a private beach. Her mother was a beautiful, kind person, but controlled every aspect of Alana's life. Wanting the best for her daughter, she was concerned about her health, her diet, her lady-like manners, and had her on an exercise and training regimen. Alana felt she was on a *short leash* because of this discipline, but her mother said it was all to build character. I sensed that Alana would enjoy spending time with our little middle class family.

Well, Crystal always treated everyone the same, which was a *problem* in this case. Later that night, after we went to bed, we started to hear strange noises from the girls' room. It sounded like someone was getting sick. Alana was forbidden to drink any soda products. When my wife went to investigate the noises, what she witnessed astonished her. The girls had sneaked two bottles of *forbidden* Mountain Dew upstairs. If that wasn't bad enough, they were taking turns drinking the soda and seeing who could burp the entire alphabet without stopping. Beryl scolded them and took the soda away. We all loved Alana and were afraid this would affect the relationship between the families. But, to this day,

Alana's mother never heard the story and we thought about changing her name in this book to keep it that way! We decided not to.

There was a time when I needed Crystal's help. We had just joined a new church in Glendale, Queens, called Christ Tabernacle. We fell in love with the church and their choir. Crystal knew how to worship. She learned it from being on the worship and praise team at Smithtown Christian School. This church worshiped differently than I was used to...I was the problem. I may have had *some* rhythm, but needed a lot more to hang in with this crew. I was so bad, when the congregation would sway right to left, I was swaying left to right, knocking people over. And because I'm a fairly good-sized man, it wasn't pretty! My other problem was I couldn't get the clapping down right. My clap usually came after everyone else already clapped. I was the one clapping on the off beat.

Since Crystal usually sat next to me, she felt she had to remedy the problem.

She told me, "When you see the person in front of you move right, you move right, when they move left, you move left."

I said, "What about the clapping?"

She said, "Just follow the person in front of you, watch and clap with them."

After a few Sundays, I was feeling pretty confident. My next challenge was wanting to sing with the choir. Never having sung in *any* church choir before, my family thought I must be losing my mind. So I said to myself, *one day, I'll show them.*

Well, that day came. We were all seated, waiting for the service to begin. My wife left the sanctuary to use the restroom, and while she was gone, Crystal and I were asked if we would like to sit with the choir during the service.

This was my chance! I responded, "Are you kidding me? We would love to sit with the choir!"

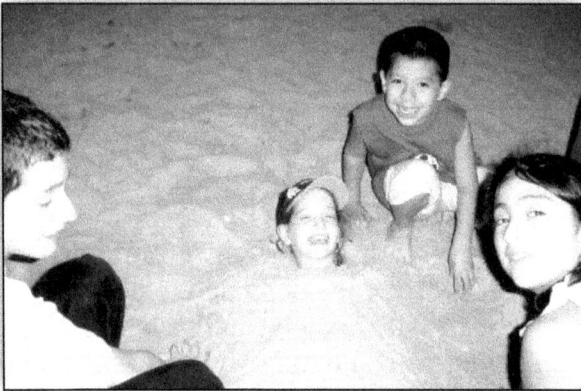

They sat me to the far left side and Crystal to the right side. As the service started, I looked out to see if I could spot my wife. When I saw her, I started jumping up and down, waving my arms side to side, and hoping she would see me with the choir. Normally, this behavior would be acceptable in this kind of church, but I was the *only one* behaving this way. The pastor kept turning around watching me. When I looked over toward Crystal, both of her hands were covering her face and her head was in her lap. I guess my overwhelming enthusiasm was a little too over-the-top for her.

When the service was over, I rushed to my wife, asking her if she saw me singing with the choir. When she said she hadn't, I couldn't believe it. I was crushed, because I thought there would never be another opportunity like that again.

One of our family's funniest stories happened after a Disney vacation. After a long, hard week of dashing from park to park, up all hours of the day and night, we came back exhausted and were getting punchy. On the plane trip back, two passengers almost got into a fist fight in the air over a seat. Then they continued arguing in the baggage area. It kind of set the tone for what was about to happen next. We had a limo driver waiting to take us home. When we met up with him, he seemed more interested in watching the two passengers argue than taking us home.

On the ride home, we all got the giggles and couldn't stop laughing. The road was covered with snow and ice. When the limo driver asked us for directions to our home, we responded by breaking out in uncontrollable laughter. It was like our family became intoxicated with laughter. Every time one of us started to speak, we all broke into laughter.

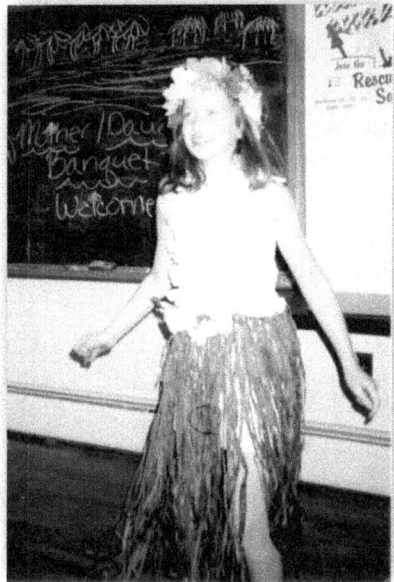

Finally, we gave the directions to the driver. When he passed the house, we started laughing again. This time he thought we were laughing at *him*, becoming angry and upset, although we didn't realize it at the time. As he made a U-turn on our street, he backed into a neighbor's car, which ignited us with laughter all over again. By this time, the limo driver had had it with our family, and ordered us out of the car. Still delirious with laughter, we watched from the driveway as he threw all our luggage over our front fence and drove away in anger, spinning his tires.

I yelled out, "You forgot the tip." The minute I said that, he went out of control and hit another neighbor's car. That was the grand finale! What a way to end a vacation!

After recovering from our vacation, my wife and I made plans to get up early in the morning and go out for breakfast. Our strategy was to sneak quietly out of the house and push the van down the street before starting the engine. We even laid out our clothes the night before, so as not to make any noise in the morning. It was a known fact that Crystal never wanted to miss anytime we went out to eat. The next morning, the plan was being executed perfectly. Beryl was behind the steering wheel as I was pushing the van down the driveway. All of a sudden, the front door opens and Crystal runs toward us in her pajamas, hops in the van yelling, "Oh, no, you don't," and refused to get out. I had to promise her we wouldn't leave without her anymore. So she got dressed and we all went to breakfast together.

There was a funny hand sign that Crystal and I used to give each other. We learned it from Marissa Miller's mother (Marissa was a good friend of Crystal's). One day, Mrs. Miller volunteered for a school class trip, and the boys were starting to make trouble. She had to go over and chastise them. After a while, the boys started acting up again, which really got Mrs. Miller ticked off. She yelled at them from a distance and sent them all a hand sign. When she got their attention, she pointed first to her eye with her index and middle finger and pointed to them with just her index finger and said, "I got my eyes on you!"

Crystal and I thought it was *so* funny! From then on, we constantly did that to each other. When Crystal was in a competition or having a tough time winning a karate bout, she would look for me in the crowd and I would give the gesture, "*I got my eyes on you,*" and it would give her the confidence to win. This was a way of reassuring her that, no matter what, we were with her and proud of her.

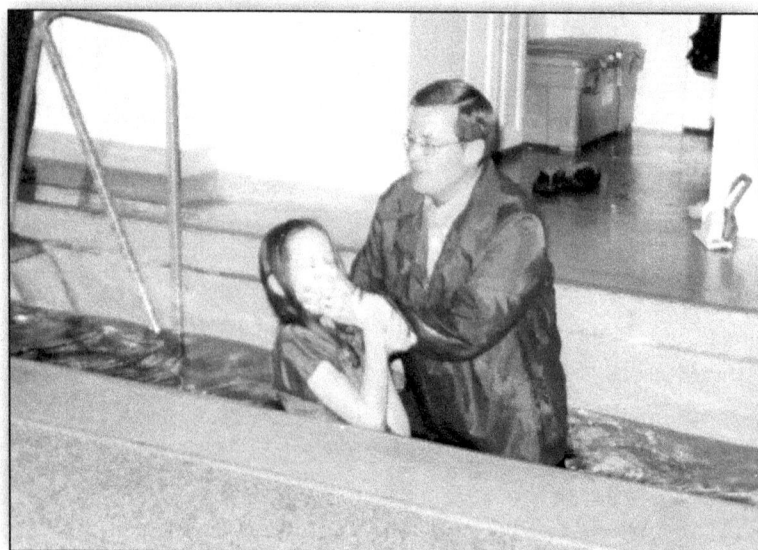

7

PASSING ON THE WISDOM

"But the wisdom that is from above is first pure, then peaceable, gentle, and easy to be intreated, full of mercy and good fruits, without partiality, and without hypocrisy." – James 3:17

As Christians, we must constantly remind ourselves that the gifts we possess belong to God for His use and for bringing glory to God. Adversaries can come in many disguises. There are those who claim to be your friend, but deep in their soul a spirit of jealousy despises you because God chose to bless you and not them. They will sometimes try to influence you, in order to control you, if they can. They can manipulate you if you let them. Their goal is to see you fail so they can step right into your shoes. A familiar New York phrase is *"beware of the back stabber."*

No person can take what God has blessed you with unless you let them. Once in a while a true friend will come along, and they will cherish the companionship with you forever. If you have one truly good friend in a lifetime, you are richly blessed. Having lived through many of these life experiences myself, I wanted to share with my children some of the trials I faced, and the knowledge I gained.

Competition can be a healthy motivator in accomplishing

goals. I always welcomed a challenge. Rivals shouldn't be viewed as enemies. The real enemy is the weakness inside of us; our inner man. Our inner spirit is revealed through training or studying. I see a competitor as someone who can help improve my skills. For me, it's never about winning or losing; it's always about doing my best. There is no shame in losing, especially if I give it my all. Victory can be measured by the ability to go the distance; where other competitors would have given up, I would finish! When tomorrow comes, it's a brand new day for starting over. Victory is still waiting for me. I've learned from my mistakes: experience is the best teacher. Never give up! This is the wisdom I have passed on to my children.

Challenges can take on different forms such as an athletic contest or academic testing, where the mind has been trained for battle through discipline. I believe in always being prepared to be victorious. Whenever a win comes by cheating or being dishonest, those actions are dishonoring to your heart. God sees everything.

In the heat of battle, I have known God's principles to be true: our strength comes from God and not ourselves. It's better than any second wind we might have ever experienced. Whatever is deposited in our hearts from God will never return void. It's heart that wins the fight, when all natural strength has been depleted.

As a family that was born competitive, we always supported each other's events. Our family philosophy was *"all for one and one for all."* It was important that we relied on each other for support. We believed that would cause us to become a closer-knit family, which it did.

Partway through elementary school, we decided that Nicholas and Crystal should shift from their public school to receive a Christian education. At 6th grade, Nicholas would switch first to the private school. We found a small and very old school that seemed like a good place to attend. Nicholas and Crystal were both tested.

Nicholas scored high on his assessment tests. At the age of 12, he was tested at a 128 IQ by the public school we attended. Crystal wasn't as high scoring on her tests, but she was more persistent in her studies and made up for it in the classroom. Crystal was on the honor roll in every school she attended. Nicholas had always struggled in the classroom with his grades. Nicholas was like one of those people I mentioned earlier who was blessed with a charismatic personality. Even his enemies liked him. One of Nicholas' greatest gifts is his humor. His likeable charm is nothing but mesmerizing. He melts the hardest heart. Teachers would tell us Nicholas had something special about him.

As time went on, we started to notice that there was a click of old-timers at school – a group stuck in the traditions of religion. It became apparent that our family came from a different Christian background, and we were considered *outsiders*. We are Christ-followers, and believe that there are no gray areas in God's Word. We take His Word literally. We reject any notion that God's spoken Word needs to be interpreted by man's reasoning. (*Colossians 2:8*) When God said thou shall not, that's not a suggestion. It's a commandment. Yesterday, today and forever, Jesus is always the same. (*Hebrews 13:8*)

As Nicholas was challenged by the *insiders* at school, he remained passionate in his faith, even at age 12. From the age of three, he would come with us when a group from church would do outreach. He won many awards for memorizing Bible Scripture in the AWANA youth group. Both Nicholas and Crystal were well-versed in the Bible from a young age.

As parents, we kept a low profile as we attended all the school functions and helped support the fundraisers. We weren't happy there, but it was better than the public school system, and at the time, we didn't know of any Christian schools of like faith. The spirit of this Christian school was one of coldness. We made a few friends through our children, but no one else went out of their way to get to know us. The Word of God was there, *but the life of the Spirit was missing.*

Little did we know the storm of religious prejudice that awaited Nicholas in the next year. Though there were never harsh words exchanged, we could tell there was an uneasy spirit between us and the governing board, which we chose to keep to ourselves. We didn't share these feelings or thoughts with others, not even the kids. We wanted to maintain a good Christian testimony, regardless of what was happening behind the scenes.

One day, the principal approached my wife and asked her if we would be better served by attending a different Christian school. Wow! Where did that come from? We privately considered it, but in the middle of the school year, it would have been tough on the children. We felt it was important for them to see their parents not running away at the first sign of controversy. In life, sometimes you have to make a stand and fight for what you believe in. Our emotions ran high, but we did not want our emotions to affect the children while they were still attending school there.

Ironically, Crystal's and Nicholas' popularity had grown to a new level. The student population was excited by their enthusiasm. During Nicholas' last year at the school, which was eighth grade, he decided to run for student council president. As his parents, we didn't have a good vibe about this, but we wanted to encourage our son in whatever he wanted to do. This would be the biggest spiritual test in his life. Would he stand up for God, or crumble and compromise? God would have to show Himself strong on Nicholas' behalf.

His opponent's parents were big financial contributors and members of the school board, with significant influence over school rules and processes. His dad was the volleyball coach, and his uncle was the Bible teacher, and the pastor of a nearby church. Having been enrolled there since kindergarten, this boy considered the school his territory. Yet, Nicholas and other classmates considered him to be a bully.

In many schools, there are parents that pull out all the stops when it comes to having their child succeed. It's a mark of prestige and leadership being a student council president, especially when elected by your peers. It makes a good impression on potential colleges, and creates career opportunities.

The campaign began.

Nicholas ran a hard campaign using fliers, tee shirts, candy bars, pens, and posters. His likeability and verbal communication connected well with the student population.

It appeared Nicholas had the lead. The momentum was going strong and he was not backing off. He could taste victory. But the *powers that be* decided this newcomer couldn't be allowed to 'steal the election.' His election posters were being removed from the school walls. His opponent's posters were the only ones left hanging. We called the school to find out what was going on. They said the posters had fallen down, and since the election was so close, there was *no need* to put them up again.

As parents, we could see where this was going. We couldn't believe that these people, who called themselves Christians, could be so unfair and participate in this vendetta against a young boy. We thought, if they were willing to tear posters down, what would happen to the counting of the votes? Election Day came. We wondered if it would be an honest process.

Nicholas spent many hours studying speeches. He especially liked the style of Ronald Reagan. His theme was '*the school is great, and I want to make it even better with the help of the students.*'

His opponent's speech was one of '*warning the students not to be fooled by someone who buys the election with candy bars and pens.*'

Nicholas concluded his speech with, *"Don't be Picky - Vote for Nicky."* As the students left the assembly hall they were chanting the slogan *"Don't be Picky - Vote for Nicky,"* as they cast their votes.

You can never predict the outcome of an election, but it sure sounded good for Nicholas. We took the day off from work to be there for him; even Grandma Eleanor Skula came. After leaving to return to work, I made my wife promise to call me with the results. She told me when Nicholas got off the school bus, his head was down like he had bad news to tell us, but then all of a sudden he leaped into the air screaming, "I won! I won!" Beryl and Crystal were jumping up and down screaming. Even though I was at work, I yelled out loud too. That night, we took the newly elected president out for a celebration dinner at his favorite Chinese restaurant.

Nicholas' victory would be short lived. His faith would be stretched and tested yet again. His leadership skills would be needed. The attacks began by the board creating a *new* rule concerning the student counsel's presidential policy. If, at any time during the school year, your grade level drops below 71%, you forfeit your presidency, and it will go to the runner up.

It was known that our family believed in the literal written scripture. Nick's Bible teacher challenged his beliefs on the accuracy of the Holy Bible in class. The teacher claimed the Bible was written by imperfect men and was subject to misinterpretation or error. Nicholas respectfully responded, by quoting a Bible verse from *Revelation 22* where God warns, *"Do not add or take away anything from this book."* As the debate went on, the students were siding with Nicholas' point of view, which angered the teacher. He was surprised at this young man's bold stand for God, who knew his Bible well, and was able to quote scripture.

The Bible teacher was trying to imply *he* was an authority on God's Word, and dismissed any other point of view. His students attended a variety of different churches, and to claim there were *no absolutes in the Word of God,* and being so sure that *the authors could have made mistakes when penning what the Holy Spirit led them to record,* was disconcerting.

When Nicholas told us what went on that day, my deeply-rooted Baptist background started to emerge. Those were fighting words to any God-fearing, born-again, Spirit-filled, blood-washed, on-fire, Jesus-loving Christian! He had drawn our son into a quarrelsome debate, and gave him a failing grade because of his stand. This teacher also failed him on a social studies exam, citing grammar errors, when in fact, all the answers were correct.

We first tried calling the Bible teacher to meet with us, and put an end to this conflict, but he wouldn't return our calls. My wife was determined to confront the man. When she spotted him at an ice cream social, he saw her walking through the crowd, and headed for the parking lot, jumped into his car, and took off. One profound thing that came out of this lesson was that we were never so proud of our son for standing up for the Gospel of Christ.

What happened next was no surprise. The *F* in Bible class caused the school board to enact their new policy to remove Nicholas from his student council presidency and replace him with their *favorite son.* We demanded an explanation and wanted to know why we weren't notified of this decision. A battle pursued when we challenged this ridiculous rule. The principal and school board saw nothing wrong with this. When I asked to see their written policy on this rule, we were told it was something that was common knowledge and there was nothing on paper; it was a verbal rule set in place, and we were told we should just accept it. Other parents wanted to know what happened. We kept it to ourselves for a while, hoping to convince them that this wasn't just wrong, it was sinful.

When the ordeal was all over, whatever school spirit we had left was gone. The will of the student body was put aside to satisfy the *powers that be*. This left a bad feeling among many families who agreed with us. Lawyer friends of ours urged us to sue the school on Nicholas' behalf. We told the school we were going to consider that option. Perhaps that would encourage some common sense. Unfortunately, there was an arrogance and pride that had been operating so long, they seemed incapable of changing. The only thing left to do was bring it before the Lord in prayer.

"Vengeance is mine." God forbids us to engage in legal action against a believer, whether they follow the will of God or not. God said, *"you're better off being wronged in this life than sue another believer, even if they're wrong."* In the end, we sent letters to all of our school friends thanking them for their prayers and support, and all of the student council members who resigned in protest over Nicholas' removal. God's Spirit was telling me to forgive them in the middle of this controversy, because if I didn't, we would become just like them.

The Lord impressed on my spirit, that my children watch me. I am their example. The last thing I wanted them to see was bitterness; so, as hard as it was, we laid it down before God's altar and let it go.

We had a feeling that God was doing something behind the scenes and our family would be blessed. Sometime later, things calmed down and returned to normal, as the school year came to a close. Three months after this incident, in an unexpected moment, tragedy struck the school. *The school volleyball coach came down with a terminal brain tumor and went home to be with the Lord without warning.* He had been a healthy man. This was the *same* family that worked so hard in getting their son elected and who later had their friends at the school become instrumental in removing Nicholas from his presidency.

Everyone was devastated. No one ever thought this could happen. Who could take the coach's place? Regardless of our differences, he did a very good job coaching the children. The controversy didn't matter anymore. It was all in vain and I wished it had never happened. If only we had known the future, we would have had Nicholas drop out of the race, so the coach could see his son elected, rather than all this drama. Our family prayed for them. We brought food to them and offered our comfort. Even though I felt there might be bitter feelings between the families, we were moved with compassion and sorrow for them.

Crystal was deeply saddened. She was one of the players on the team and never experienced losing anyone before. I often wonder to myself, was it worth it? All that time we spent fighting to position ourselves. *Maybe the lesson missed was we took our eyes off Jesus,* just for a moment, and now it took a season of grieving to unite our spirits before God. I was reminded that the greatest characteristic you can have in your life is love.

After graduation in June, we never returned to that school again. They have tried to reach out to us, but God led us to a new Christian school where we were blessed beyond measure. We have seen that when we find ourselves in the wilderness, God always leads us out of the situation.

8

YEARS OF JUBILEE

"For it is the jubilee; it shall be holy unto you: ye shall eat the increase thereof out of the field." –Leviticus 25:12

There is a period in a person's life when you enjoy remembering the *glory years*. Just the thought of reliving old memories can return me to a happier time. Memories will last a lifetime and the love we've shared with people on earth are the only things we can bring with us to Heaven. When we were the center of our children's world, they would look to us for a nod of approval. It is worth all the hard work that went into raising them. We gave them our very best; putting our whole hearts into molding them. And then a sad day eventually comes when we can no longer be there for them...

Many times we think *if only* I could return to relive the past, holding back on that damaging word spoken, or correcting that wrong decision...Personal experience can show us that sometimes winning a battle can cost us the war in life. Life itself can be too short. As life moves on, all we seem to recall are the happier times; a different place that our mind takes us to, erasing negative thoughts from the past. The arguments weren't worth all the fighting over. In the end, it is the love of family that really matters.

When we visit my mother-in-law at the nursing home, it just breaks my heart. I can't help but look around and see *"the greatest generation ever born"* wasting away right before my eyes. Wasted volumes of advice is sitting there, in every room, week after week. I wonder what knowledge and wisdom is locked inside their minds. What happened to all their loved ones? Have they forgotten to visit them? When did they lose their value in society and with their loved ones? Somewhere their children lost their way, or perhaps forgot the lessons they were taught. Where did their love go? The parent-child roles have reversed, and, in the care and nurturing role, we sometimes take our parents for granted. If only the younger generation would have been wiser in taking their advice. Lessons don't always have to be learned the hard way. Good advice, acted upon, can avoid a lot of trouble. I've always encouraged my children to seek wise counsel, in my absence, from older and wiser people. (*Proverbs 16:16*) *"Wisdom is better than gold."*

One of the wisest decisions our family has ever made was actually made by Crystal. We were asking God's spirit to lead us in finding a new Christian school for Nicholas. It was best for our family to have him move on from his current school. During our search, we came to a school called the Smithtown Christian School. We had visited there once before but had forgotten it even existed.

When we first pulled up to the school, Crystal and Nicholas were both impressed. The school is affiliated with a great church, the Smithtown Gospel Tabernacle. Not knowing what to expect, Beryl and Nicholas walked briskly in front of us as we headed inside to the appointment we had set up. Crystal and I were right behind them, observing everything for the first time. As we were walking hand in hand, it was as though the Spirit of God came upon us. Crystal froze in place. She began pulling my hand to stop me. She cupped her hands to my ear and whispered, "Dad, if Nicholas doesn't want to come here, I definitely do!"

She was mesmerized and I was overwhelmed, not expecting to see a Christian school with this kind of grandeur. I couldn't disagree with her. This place was filled with God's greatness, and it was just what we needed!

There were still hurdles to overcome; Nicholas and Crystal had to be accepted first. Two criteria had to be addressed; the school wanted to know where you stood academically and spiritually. A certain academic level was necessary to achieve success. The whole family was called in to undergo a thorough screening process. The interviewers needed to know if Nicholas and Crystal *wanted* to be there.

Toward the end of the interview, we were told we would be notified with the results by mail, which didn't sound too promising. They must have been able to see the disappointment on all our faces when hearing that, because a second examiner slipped by saying, "Have a good summer and *we'll see you in September.*" After hearing those words of encouragement, we all clicked our heels for joy.

Soon after the interviews, we received a letter congratulating us. This was the victory our family had prayed for! As we prepared Nicholas and Crystal for their new school, a lot more would be expected from them. There was a dress code that required school uniforms and a standard of Christian behavior that was to be exhibited at all times. Their purpose was to raise a godly standard among the student population. Their conduct was also to prepare them professionally, so when they started their careers, they would have a godly foundation.

When school started, there was an excitement in our house, and a little angst, not knowing what to expect. We knew the teachers and staff would be friendly, but we weren't too sure about our children being accepted by the other students. There was a lot of prayer that summer for the upcoming year.

Our prayers were answered. Nicholas and Crystal were treated as celebrities from day one. They had become overnight sensations. The Lord not only answered our prayers, but poured out a blessing on their lives like none we had ever seen before.

Nicholas was more outgoing than his sister. It wasn't long before he was praising his teachers and talking about new friends he made. Invitations for sleepovers and birthday parties were coming daily from his classmates and they were reaching out by the dozens. Nicholas was being blessed by God, and flourishing where God had planted him.

Crystal, on the other hand, was slow to build relationships. She was still a shy, quiet, and reserved person. Even though she possessed an aggressive, competitive spirit, she wouldn't initiate a conversation unless she knew you well. She was signing up for every event that she could. It wasn't long before she was everywhere; the school band, the choir, plays, musicals, and worship dancing. Slowly, Crystal's popularity started to grow and then overnight she got *discovered*. Her classmates were interested in finding out more about her. It really had no effect on her ego at all, though she was never the same again. She had always been a loner and we were all taken aback by this new attention she was receiving.

One day, Crystal's new school friends wanted her to join the praise team, but there was one small problem: tryouts were over and the praise team members were already chosen. They had already started working on a new project. In an effort to sneak Crystal in, her friends all huddled around in a group and marched onto the stage, hiding her from the teacher. This was definitely out of character for our daughter!

As the practice began, the teacher noticed something was not right! The girls giggled and then the teacher realized that Crystal wasn't part of the team. She asked Crystal her name. Crystal remained quiet. She was really scared and it wasn't so funny anymore. There was dead silence; the fear of getting in serious trouble had become a reality. No one had the courage to raise their voice on Crystal's behalf, except for one. One of the girls yelled out, "She really loves to sing and can sing well!"

The teacher looked Crystal right in the eye and asked this question:

"Do you think you're good enough to sing with us?"

She paused for a moment and modestly answered, "Yes."

"Are you willing to stay after school to practice with us?"

She replied, "Yes."

Then the teacher replied, "Welcome to the praise team." The girls let out a scream of joy and welcomed Crystal to the team.

Every Tuesday after school the choir had to rehearse for Wednesdays, when they held chapel and led the student body in a youth worship service. Crystal was faithful to this team, but she was not one for telling her parents what was going on in school. We had no idea she had joined!

Beryl had to come to the church for an unrelated matter, but as she walked down the hallway, she heard worship music. Curious, she slipped into the back of the sanctuary. When she realized Crystal was singing with the worship team, she couldn't hold back her tears of joy. Never expecting to see this, it was a memory etched in my wife's mind that will live forever. My only regret was that I was not there to see that.

Nicholas and Crystal's loyalty would again be put to a test.

They both shared a similar nature of coming to the defense of the weak and a sense of right and wrong.

One mid-summer day late in the afternoon, my family was bored, so we decided to go out for the evening and do something different. Business at the family mechanic shop was slow, so we agreed to close the doors early for the day. Beryl and the kids came to pick me up. Suddenly, I noticed a couple of thieves across the parking lot breaking into a customer's vehicle. They were right in the midst of stealing a CD player. I let out a shout and it wasn't long before they were exposed.

The thieves were caught red-handed and everyone's reactions were keyed up as the thieves took off, trying to escape. Without hesitation, a vigorous chase began. They had the jump on me, but I wasn't about to give up on capturing them. An adrenaline rush was now taking over my body. As I started to gain on them, my peripheral vision spotted something and my head whipped to the right. It was Crystal in full sprint, starting to pass me by! Although my intentions were to handle this myself, I had raised the children to never to run from a fight, to stick up for each other and protect the weak.

Everyone was now involved in the chase. Nicholas was right behind us. I always told my children to welcome a challenge, but in this case, wisdom was needed. Emotion was now making the decisions my head should have made. I was afraid the situation might turn violent. I called off the pursuit before things became risky.

Righteous indignation took over in Crystal and Nicholas. They were refusing to stop. Finally the pursuit ended, but their passion was now directed towards me. Anger and frustration had taken control and no one was thinking straight. All the kids kept saying was, "We could have had them! We were in striking distance! We can't believe you're going to let them get away with this after seeing what they did to that car."

They were like hungry warriors that had trained their whole life waiting for a time like this to happen. And now I was being blamed for robbing them of their opportunity to inflict justice.

"What was the purpose for all the intense karate training?" they wondered. Of course it was not to kill and maim, but to be able to survive any situation they would face in life.

"I will study and get ready and someday my chance will come." -Abraham Lincoln

In an effort to calm them down, they needed to know that God had seen everything, and He would get them *Himself*. Even so, they still felt they were justified and cheated out of their chance to correct a wrong.

I couldn't let them be judge, jury, and executioner. Both Nicholas and Crystal had been taking *full contact* karate lessons, three times a week for over five years and been put through some of the most brutal combat fighting there was. There was no question in my mind what might have happened if we'd caught up with those thugs.

They both showed a courageous spirit, and truthfully, I was never more proud of them than on that day. When the incident was all over, we had to remember whose Spirit was controlling us. A lesson well learned.

Our family had come together in a moment of truth, and we had taken action, for which they both proved worthy. As for me, God filled me with the pride and joy of my children. It was a blessed time of my life that will forever be etched in my heart.

The children inherited their humility from their mother. Beryl is a quiet, gentle soul who speaks from her heart. Her greatest gift from God is her kindness.

Many times I've witnessed acts Beryl did in secret, like

blessing people with home cooked meals. Devoted to God's work, she never complained and was always eager to put others first, and at times with great sacrifice. During a time when we were financially struggling, another family was really hurting. Beryl made her special dish, two baked Ziti pasta meals, one for us and the other for this family. One Ziti was loaded with meat, which I love, and the other was just plain. Guess who got the better one? You guessed it...the *other* family. That's my wife's generous heart.

Another time, a single woman in our church lost all her personal belongings after her house burned down. There was no money in our budget to give her and that disturbed my wife. She was determined to help this devastated woman. Beryl found out she needed a blanket and we had recently bought a new blanket set for ourselves. My wife said God was telling her to give the new blanket set to the sister in need.

She sent countless cards and letters of encouragement, visited lonely people, spending hours sitting with them.

Another gift which Beryl, Nicholas and Crystal all share is that no matter where they went, children were drawn to them.

Despite the different attributes Beryl and I have, God gave Nicholas and Crystal exactly what He needed them to have to serve His purposes. For a while I was concerned that Crystal had become too much of a daddy's girl, and that my influence may cause her to be a *tom-boy*. But, Beryl has always been a good mother and role model. So, I was glad to hear Crystal tell her mother one day that when she grew up, she wanted to be just like her. Praise God! Hearing that soothed my soul.

as a Mother's Day present
Crystal drew a chalk drawing

9

ALL SEEMS WELL AS CAN BE

"So that we may boldly say, The Lord is my helper, and I will not fear what man shall do unto me." –Hebrews 13:6

It was October of 2001, and all of us here in New York were still reeling from the 9/11 terrorist attacks. People were deeply hurting. Our country was at war, struck by people we never knew. They hated us because of our faith and way of life. It was called a holy war, but we didn't notice anything holy about it.

We decided to go to Disney World in Florida for a family vacation. We felt like we were the only guests in the entire park. People were still traumatized and afraid to travel. It was strangely empty and odd for there to be no lines at the rides.

But, life for us as a family during 2001 was really great. Nicholas and Crystal were doing very well in school. Their friends and teachers really loved them. Crystal took advantage of every school activity available to her: singing, dancing, ballet, band, plays, cheer leading, karate, and more. Despite all of these time-consuming activities, she still made the honor roll. Some thought it was just too much to do, but Crystal was an extremely high-energy person.

Crystal very rarely got sick. She would catch a cold one day and the next day, it was gone. Maybe all the rigorous martial arts training conditioned her physically, mentally, and emotionally. She was in the best physical shape of her life. All those push-ups, sit-ups, heavy bag training, and running that were part of her training paid off. As her Dad, I wanted her to be prepared for any challenge in life that came her way. She was becoming a female warrior.

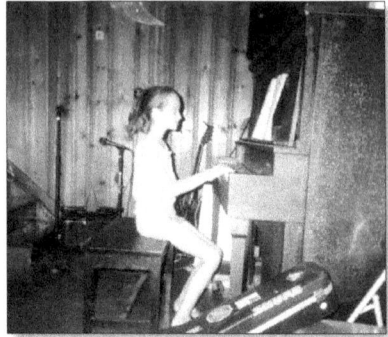

Crystal very rarely shed tears over herself. When she experienced pain, she was taught to work through it. However, she would get upset when she saw others being hurt or suffering. Crystal learned from her faith in God to put others first, before herself. Crystal considered herself blessed by God. We would soon experience the greatest test of our family's faith. *It would be God's strength that would be made perfect in our weakness.*

One day, we received a phone call from the school nurse, explaining that Crystal had an excruciating headache. Beryl picked her up from school and brought her to the pediatrician. He thought it was nothing, and it would pass. Later that night, the pain got worse. Something was wrong and whatever this was, it was out of the ordinary.

Later on, we found out that Crystal wasn't eating her lunch and she was having trouble climbing the stairs at school. She had to stop half way up and catch her breath. Our whole family started praying for her. We took her to the hospital to be examined. For a while, no one was able to give us any answers. We soon realized *they* would not be able to help us. After taking x-rays and tests, they led me and Beryl into a private room and told us that Crystal had a *large* tumor on her brain. We would have to take her to another hospital that specialized in child brain tumors and was equipped to handle this kind of procedure.

At this point, my wife started to faint.

We needed to draw strength from God right away. Hearing news like that is like getting hit directly in the stomach. Whatever strength we thought we had, it was gone; and for a short while, we felt so alone. We needed to start calling people we knew, but for a moment in time, we were still in shock and speechless.

One of the first people we called was Sheila Foerth, a close friend and a leader of the local chapter of "*Moms In Prayer International.*" My wife was a member of her group. She immediately started a prayer chain that spanned worldwide.

Meanwhile, Crystal and I left in the ambulance to go to Schneider's Children's Hospital. My wife drove back to our house to pick up Nicholas at 2:00 in the morning. Concerned they would get lost, they actually arrived at the hospital ahead of us. When my cell phone rang, it was Nicholas wanting to know where we were. We were in the lobby working on the admission process for Crystal. We were greeted by a mob of all kinds of doctors at 3:00 a.m. Saturday morning. Within minutes, the team of doctors were strategizing and attending to Crystal's needs.

On Saturday afternoon, all the tests were complete. The lead brain surgeon spoke to us about the operation scheduled for Sunday morning. Things were moving too fast for us. Brain surgery? We had barely grasped the realization of the diagnosis. We told the doctor in charge we would like to get a second opinion. Doctor Mittler, one of the top pediatric surgeons in the country, told us that if we didn't operate immediately, Crystal may not make it.

I told the doctor we have another problem. Our insurance company, Oxford Insurance, is denying the claim.

The doctor said, "That's no surprise, they only like two kinds of patients – well and dead."

I really didn't need to hear that comment, but the doctor assured us that his office would take care of the problem, and, unlike insurance companies, *he* cared for his little patients.

Crystal was heavily sedated and they made her as comfortable as possible. In the meantime, we had a meeting with all the doctors to discuss the effects of the surgery. They told us several things; Crystal may not survive the operation; or if she did, she could go into a vegetative state. Another outcome is that she could become paralyzed on her left side because the tumor was on the right side of her brain. The least that will occur is her personality may change. Confident God would heal her, I asked, *"Change it for the better?"* The doctor was puzzled by my question, but I felt it was necessary to break the tension for my wife. Beryl laughed. It was a private joke among our family. You have to have known Crystal's personality to appreciate the joke. As we walked out of the room, not realizing the seriousness of the situation, we both thought this was some kind of cruel nightmare we were having.

There was no time to waste and we knew it was time to storm heaven. "Let's get a prayer chain going," was our consensus. We personally called every Christian we knew and every church we could think of. This was our *only* way of fighting back.

I prayed silently, *"God, my God, I need to speak to my doctor Jesus in heaven; this is an emergency!"* All appears to be an island of despair with no help in sight. We were too scared to cry because we knew that once we started, we wouldn't be able to stop, and we did not want Crystal to see us upset or weak in our faith.

That first night, we all slept in Crystal's hospital room; me, Beryl, and Nicholas. It was against the hospital rules, but a nurse showed us compassion and let us stay. During the night, Crystal had to use the restroom, but she was hooked up to an IV stand and the hospital wanted the bed pan to be used. Crystal wasn't about to do that. She got up from her bed and made her way over to the bathroom, as we all tried to stop her. I even stood in front of the bathroom door to block her from going in. I am about 250 and 5'-10' tall and Crystal weighed ninety pounds. She reached around me with her arm and pushed me out of the way, and I landed, thank God, on an empty bed. We were all shocked. Where did she get all that strength from? After that, Crystal slept like a baby for the rest of the night.

Later that night, a terrible thought came to me: What would happen if the Lord would call Crystal home? Not wanting to even think like that, I focused on the good things God blessed us with. I recalled happier times with my daughter. One fun thing Crystal and I would do together was go shopping for food early in the morning before school started. We would leave the house about 6:00 a.m. and race to the market, in order to get back home before she missed the school bus. We would run down the aisles of the supermarket, throwing everything we could think of in the cart. Crystal probably came with me just to make sure she got her favorite foods, but I didn't mind at all. Matter of fact, I enjoyed her company. My mind meditated on these good times.

A night of praying made way for the morning. They came for Crystal with the gurney, and I wished things could be different. This was the first time in years that we wouldn't be in church on a Sunday morning. As they were preparing Crystal for the surgery, Crystal could tell her mother was very upset. Crystal, trained as a warrior and sensitive to her mother's needs, had reassured her Mom everything was going to be alright.

As the team started to roll Crystal away, she called her mom over and whispered in a weak voice, "Don't be sad; the worst that could happen to me is I'll be with Jesus sooner than later!"

Not the best thing to tell your mother before going in for brain surgery, but that's Crystal's daring attitude. At the age of eleven, Crystal was mentally quite mature. She knew what she wanted in life and was not afraid to go after it. But as soon as the doors closed and they took Crystal into the operating room, we all wept out loud. I broke down and wept for my little Crystal. We all felt alone in a crowd of strangers, all faceless, and concerned with their own burdens. It felt like God forgot to send a Comforter to us in our time of need. There was no one there for us in that moment of misery.

But God is faithful. He sent us an angel in human form, Coach Kogut, Crystal's cheer leading coach at the Smithtown Christian School. She was the type of person who knew how to encourage us; she was just what the doctor ordered. She told us she had a dream the night before, and God spoke to her and kept putting Crystal's face before her. So, instead of going to church that morning, she drove all the way to the hospital to be with us. We really didn't know her all that well, but after talking to her for the next several hours, we discovered that she attended the same church as us, and our children all attended Smithtown Christian School together.

Later that day, family and friends started showing up by the dozens. We received a good report from Smithtown Gospel Tabernacle. The senior pastor, Gary Zarlengo, called the congregation to prayer. He said, "One of our sixth grade students was rushed to the hospital. She is eleven years old and about to undergo emergency brain surgery. The doctors are not sure of the outcome, whether she will survive the operation or not. There's a chance she could become paralyzed. We are going to pray and believe God right now for a miracle."

After making that announcement from the pulpit, most of the congregation fell to their knees and prayed. This was good news to our hearts. Other Christians from other churches were doing the same. Many believers from across America lifted up prayers for Crystal in their houses of worship.

Soon, the lobby was filling up with family and church friends. It got so overwhelming, we tried to separate into small groups in order to give the appearance we were not at all connected in any way. It didn't really work well. When Dr. Mittler came to give his report about Crystal's condition, a large mob of people surrounded him. What finally blew our cover was when the crowd started questioning him about the operation and how Crystal was doing. It looked like a news conference. Every one cheered when the operation was announced as a success. Dr. Mittler added he was cautiously optimistic, and was uncertain about any future complication because it would take a couple of days to see if any brain damage had occurred. The doctor wasn't sure if the tumor was cancerous. At one point, Dr. Mittler had enough of the questions, and ordered the crowd of guests to leave the hospital.

Crystal wasn't out of the woods yet. She was moved from the operating room into the recovery room. As we slowly entered the room, there was an uncertainty about what we would see. She was sleeping and had a bandage wrapped around her head. We didn't know if she had become paralyzed on her right side, or if she would be able to use that side at all. When Crystal came to, she picked up her right hand to reach for her mother to hug her. She had a smile of joy when she saw her family around her. *We just witnessed our first answer to prayer. Hallelujah! Praise our Lord.*

Meanwhile, Crystal's friends and classmates were very concerned about their friend. They left nothing to chance.

Someone made a flyer of Crystal's face, and typed in the words "*Pray for Crystal*" and taped them all over the school and church walls. Every time the class period would change, groups of the students from Smithtown Christian School would gather over the flyers, lay hands on Crystal's picture, and pray together.

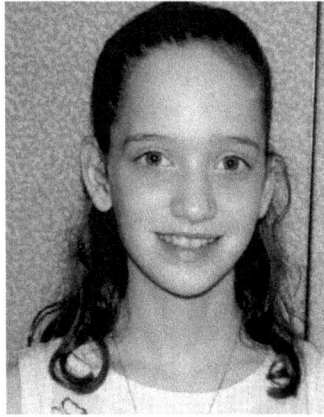

Crystal Skula

Crystal's family would like to
thank all of <u>you</u>,
Crystal's dear friends at
Smithtown Christian School,
for your prayers and love.

God is good! And He loves us all!

We were ecstatic to hear about all the children praying for Crystal's healing. Not long after, Pastor Salvatore Greco and his wife Josie came to the hospital and prayed over Crystal. Pastor Greco is the education pastor in charge of the school.

He told Crystal, "I am going to read Psalm 41 over your life."

Psalm 41

1 *Blessed is he that considereth the poor: the Lord will deliver him in time of trouble.*

2 *The Lord will preserve him, and keep him alive; and he shall be blessed upon the earth: and thou wilt not deliver him unto the will of his enemies.*

3 *The Lord will strengthen him upon the bed of languishing: thou wilt make all his bed in his sickness.*

4 *I said, Lord, be merciful unto me: heal my soul; for I have sinned against thee.*

5 *Mine enemies speak evil of me, when shall he die, and his name perish?*

6 *And if he come to see me, he speaketh vanity: his heart gathereth iniquity to itself; when he goeth abroad, he telleth it.*

7 *All that hate me whisper together against me: against me do they devise my hurt.*

8 *An evil disease, say they, cleaveth fast unto him: and now that he lieth he shall rise up no more.*

9 *Yea, mine own familiar friend, in whom I trusted, which did eat of my bread, hath lifted up his heel against me.*

10 *But thou, O Lord, be merciful unto me, and raise me up, that I may requite them.*

11 *By this I know that thou favourest me, because mine enemy doth not triumph over me.*

12 *And as for me, thou upholdest me in mine integrity, and set me before thy face forever.*

13 *Blessed be the Lord God of Israel from everlasting, and to everlasting. Amen, and Amen.*

"Crystal, you may not know what this means, but God spoke it, and now we're going to believe it's going to apply to your life. I am going to ask God for a blessing on your life."

Five days after being admitted to the hospital, Crystal was on her way home. Not long after we brought her home with us, she was already planning to perform in a dance recital a week later.

Crystal was about to graduate from the sixth grade in a month's time. I guess five days in bed was too much for her; it was time to start living again. The whole family came out to see Crystal at her dance recital, including her grandparents. She looked beautiful that night. No one would ever believe that just one week earlier, she underwent brain surgery! Her coordination was never affected at all; it was like she was treated for a mosquito bite. No one could convince us God wasn't with us during our time of trouble.

A couple of weeks later was graduation. Usually, it would be just another school event to attend, but this one would be different. We would be in the presence of all those beautiful people who prayed, fasted and blessed our family with so many gifts of love. When we entered the pavilion, you could actually feel the love all around us, as people viewed a miracle from God. All our Christian brothers and sisters surrounded Crystal, thanking God for His mercy and truth. It almost felt like a piece of Heaven came down here to earth. That special day will stay etched in our hearts forever. During the award ceremony, when Crystal went forward to receive her diploma, I thanked God in my heart for making

this day possible.

We were all proud of what a godly young lady Crystal had become. She embodied all the godly lessons we had taught her, and the martial arts training had prepared Crystal's character for a day like this. Jesus Christ was first and foremost in her life and He was standing by her in the fiery trial she had just passed through. She never shed a tear through the whole ordeal. I wish I could say the same for myself.

After a couple months of healing, we had to return to the hospital for further treatments. The results came in, weeks later; Crystal's brain tumor was called glioblastoma, a multiform stage-four *cancer*.

Most patients don't know the living God like we do. When we left and started walking back to the car, Crystal stopped me and told me she had been diagnosed with the "C" word. Someone in the hospital decided to tell Crystal about her life expectancy. It came as a surprise to us, since we had no idea what they told her. We were all hoping it would only be a non-cancerous brain tumor.

Crystal said, "Dad, they told me I have brain cancer."

I replied, "Crystal! You let them say anything they want! Our Doctor lives in Heaven and until He tells us otherwise, we will wait for His answer. So you tell them they can call it anything they want, but they better never, ever call you late for dinner." She laughed and we decided it was time to get something to eat.

For the next several weeks, she had to undergo radiation treatments. The radiation people designed a mesh mask that was made out of what looked like fiber glass. It was bolted to the table, and while being treated, you couldn't move your head. The only good thing about this was you could bring your own music to play during the session. That was great because Crystal had to learn a bunch of songs. She was going to be in a gospel musical and had a lead part.

Some of the lasting results were that Crystal would, in this case, lose all of her natural hair, never to grow back, according to the doctors. This upset her because God had blessed her with beautiful hair. The hospital workers told Crystal that short term memory loss was expected next. We told Crystal we'd heard this all before, and to remember the doctor's first predictions; you might not survive the operation, and if you did, you'd probably be paralyzed on your right side. The doctor even told us your personality would change, and we were hoping it might.

Crystal responded to my teasing with an exasperated, "Dad!"

"Well, all I'm saying is, if God can see you through all of this, He can restore your hair back to you in the future. That's nothing for Almighty God."

The first treatments were like nothing, but after a while, they took their toll on Crystal, and us. The good thing was that she was in a musical at her church and needed to learn her singing parts. The radiation people let her play her music while having to lay still and undergo her treatments.

Crystal eventually lost her hair, but wasn't too concerned about it. She was able to find some wigs that were a perfect match with her color. People couldn't even tell she was wearing a wig, it looked so natural. By mid-August, we were finished with the radiation treatments.

But the worst was yet to come; chemotherapy. There was a new kind of chemotherapy that worked well in adults, and they were starting to use it on children. We thought it sounded good. It was to be administered in pill form. After watching Crystal taking this, I felt like we were giving her poison. It was hell on earth to see her going through this treatment. When it was over, she dropped twenty pounds off her already small frame and looked horrible. She was weak and her body needed to be built back up. That's when we started feeding Crystal her favorite meals and lots of ice cream; *anything* she wanted. We even had a weekly tab with the ice cream truck and deli-man. Despite everything Crystal had to endure, there was never a *"why me"* or *"poor me"* attitude from her.

After completing her chemotherapy, Crystal started experiencing terrible back pain. Her mother took her to our local pediatrician. He gave us a ridiculous diagnosis. He stated Crystal's spine was damaged from the radiation. We had to take it a step further and keep investigating. After getting an x-ray from Zwanger-Pesiri, they told us (off the record) they didn't see any damage. The local pediatrician didn't have a clue what was going on. Next stop was Schneider's Children's Hospital in New Hyde Park, Long Island.

After getting settled in, an elderly doctor walked in and said hello to Crystal. She replied hello, and he asked, "What's wrong?" So, she told the doctor about her back pain.

He said, "You see those bumps on your arms?"

Crystal said, "Yes."

"You have what's called shingles! Matter of fact, I have them too," then he lifted up his sleeves and showed us his shingles. The only bad news was that Crystal had to be isolated for a few days in the hospital room, and only one family member could stay with her. Beryl was exhausted, so she and Nicholas went home for some sleep. I volunteered to spend the weekend with Crystal. We watched movies and played board games the whole weekend. It was a lot of fun and we made the best out of a bad situation. I sneaked out and brought McDonald's and ice cream to her.

Tutors for Crystal's schoolwork were called in so she could catch up with her classmates. She lost most of the seventh grade because of her treatments, but God had some surprises coming soon.

One morning, out of the blue, we received a telephone call from the Children's Brain Tumor Foundation. Because of Crystal's incredible outlook on her condition, she was picked to be interviewed and taped by a film crew from Paramount pictures. They set up a room in the New York City Hilton Hotel, to film a couple of children. When it came time for Crystal's turn, she started telling her testimony on camera. We weren't sure how it would be received. One thing we knew for sure was that Crystal would give her Lord and Savior all the glory and honor He deserved for healing her and making her well.

A strange event was about to take place; my wife and Crystal were the last family to be interviewed that day. Covered in prayer, we were ready. Crystal gave her testimony on how she put her faith in the hands of the Lord and wasn't afraid to meet her God.

After the interview ended, all the film crew broke down weeping. Most of them weren't believers, but they were able to see God in this young, confident girl. They didn't understand what had happened. We recognized that God was using this illness to bring Himself glory. God gave us faith and we knew her life was firmly in His hands.

10

THE UNFINISHED CHAPTER

"Now faith is the substance of things hoped for, the evidence of things not seen." –Hebrews 11:1

Courage Beyond Measure

Because of large hospital bills, we found ourselves stuck in a financial rut with our backs up against the wall. There was only one way out: fight our way through it. We needed to focus on Crystal's health and getting her well. It was 2004, and we were approaching the three year mark from her brain operation. We were told by doctors that most children didn't last six months with this particular type of brain cancer. Of course, they didn't realize Crystal was an extraordinary person with faith in an extraordinary God. Courage and fearlessness were built into this quiet young girl, which our family's faith had instilled in her. Crystal was on a mission. She had a lot of lost time to catch up on, and she wasn't going to allow any kind of challenge to go by without completing it.

We were on vacation, in Yorktown, Virginia. Our family had just arrived, and our bags weren't even unpacked when Crystal hit us with this: a 5-K race was coming up on July 4, 2004, and she wanted to enter it. We tried to talk her out of competing since she really hadn't trained for it. We were concerned she may not have the strength. She had just finished her radiation and chemotherapy treatments, and lost thirty pounds. Gaining the weight back was a slow process. Crystal had a strong spirit and nothing was going to stop her. To make a long story short, she entered the race and finished second to last, only beating out a 91-year-old woman! Crystal laughed! She was just happy to *finish* the race. They gave her a medal, especially when they found out she was a cancer survivor.

The spring of 2005 was very good for our family. Crystal was doing incredibly well, especially in her dance class. She had just been offered the lead part of Clair in the Nutcracker play for Christmas, and was going to be trained by professional ballerinas from Germany. When we heard the news, we were ecstatic and jumped for joy. The dance studio gave Crystal a training video to study for the part. No matter how she felt, she always made sure she found the strength to dance. It was her passion and it kept her looking forward.

Crystal wasn't afraid to die. Living was the hard part. Normally, she took her training very seriously, but this time *all* she had to run on was pure heart. She knew her eternal destiny. Life was made to live and Crystal was determined to live it to the fullest. Nicholas was graduating from Smithtown Christian School. We were thanking God that his day had finally arrived.

Even though we still had our problems, life was moving forward. We knew we needed to focus on the important things in life for our children. They were becoming adults. Crystal was 13...going on 30, and Nicholas was 17. Now at the end of his senior year, he was enjoying his new-found freedom. Their lives were being transformed right before our eyes. Their futures were filled with hopes and dreams.

They had developed a nice social network of peers. It was hard to keep track of their many relationships. It was good to see our children doing so well in life. Crystal was becoming more assertive, too. During the Christmas season, she insisted that the family drive to Rockefeller Center to see the Christmas

tree and ice skaters. All of us were shocked to see her becoming so demanding about her desires.

We decided to fulfill her wishes and go visit the holiday sites. We even miraculously found a legal parking spot right in front of the tree in Rockefeller Center! That was divine favor from God! First we went for a tour of NBC Studios. As our family walked closer to view the tree, it was like we were in a movie set. It started to snow right before us. We asked a couple from Iowa to take our picture. This picture-perfect scene was like what my wife refers to as a "Heaven wink."

Another incident I will never forget occurred one day when Crystal and I planned to go to the mall by ourselves. Prior to leaving, Beryl and I got into a heated argument, which *rarely* happened. The tension was high and it left my wife upset. As Crystal and I were walking through the parking lot, she stopped dead in her tracks, and turned her face to mine.

She said, "Dad, I want to talk to you about something! You don't know this, but when you argue with Mom, you hurt her feelings and make her cry. You don't see this, but I do. Dad, I want you to make me a promise that you won't hurt Mom like that anymore."

I immediately felt convicted and promised Crystal I would take her advice. I've often wondered since if she was trying to prepare us. *Did she know something we didn't?*

Crystal was eager to visit with family and friends we hadn't seen in a while. She had a great grand-mom Skula and great grandfather that lived in Surprise County in upstate New York. She also had two other grandmothers and a grandfather that she loved very much. She loved all the farm animals and the open land in that area. I knew she needed a change of scenery. I told many stories about all the good times we spent on the farm, when her great grandfather was younger, and how we would work the fields bringing the hay bales into the barn. The amount of hay we brought in would feed the cows all winter long.

One day I took Crystal to work with me. We stopped at the bank and they were having a contest. They wanted you to put your name in a box and the winner would win a huge tray of candy.

Crystal wanted to do it and I said, "No, you never win those kinds of things. It's a waste of time."

She said, "Come on Dad, it's worth a try!"

Now the tellers in the bank started to come to her defense yelling, "Come on, Dad! It's free. It's worth a try."

So we put our name in the box. The next day, we got a call from the bank telling us Crystal won the prize, and she could come and pick up her candy box. I always wondered if those tellers in the bank fixed that contest.

Crystal was starting to regain her weight and physical strength. I was still privately praying that God would perform a miracle in her life and restore her natural, beautiful hair – that the radiation doctor said would never ever grow back – and cover those ugly scars. We were going to wait on the Lord, because He is our healer. But, because of her natural-looking wig, Crystal seemed content with that.

From time-to-time, I worked another job on the side

training dogs at people's homes. Crystal always loved coming along with me. She loved dogs and was great interacting with them. She would help me train them in learning obedience. She was blessed with a sweet touch, and they responded better to her than me. Maybe she was a *dog whisperer*. Of course, I had to pay Crystal for her hard work. When it came to money I owed her, she held my feet to the fire!

There were times that people would ask Beryl the most outrageous, bizarre questions imaginable, like, "How could God allow this to happen to you and your family?"

She would answer, "Why not?"

If Crystal got this question, we told her to answer saying, "To have a good testimony, you have to pass a test. Only the ones that God feels worthy enough to be tested in this manner will be promoted to a higher service, and God held me in high esteem to be worthy of His testing."

Before we knew it, Nicholas was getting ready to start college and Crystal was going to begin high school. She was previously tutored by two of her teachers from Smithtown Christian School, John and Agnes Contes. God bless them...they would volunteer their services, free of charge. This couple was what we called the *real deal*. They lived like the believers right out of the book of James. They were doers of the Word, and not just talkers. Later on in life, we had the privilege and honor of becoming their personal friends. The Contes family was totally sold out for the Lord. We were encouraged and inspired by their walk with God.

Then, something else started to change in our lives.

In the midst of all we were going through with Crystal, a legal battle over our property with my brother had come to a head. In order to avoid the house going to the auction block, we had finally reached a deal. We were able to refinance the house and pay off my brother and start another 30-year mortgage. But, our new mortgage payment tripled. On September 15, Beryl and I were sitting inside our attorney's office, making payments for all our legal fees and to creditors in order to save our home. After all was said and done, we had less than a thousand dollars left to our name.

Beryl and I were planning to stop for a late lunch to celebrate an end to this nightmare situation with my brother. However, as soon as we were finished with the attorney, we received a phone call from Crystal telling us to please come home. She said she was not feeling well. It came as a surprise, so we canceled our plans and raced home. We brought her in to the doctor, and he recommended that we go right to the hospital. They took an x-ray and found a large tumor on the *other* side of her brain. This tumor was *much* larger than the first one.

Not wanting to accept this news, we started praying. "Lord we need your help..."

When we got to the operating area, a new doctor was there. He didn't want to operate; telling us the best thing for Crystal and our family was to let her expire and not risk the chance of her becoming a vegetable for the rest of her life. A rage was building up in my soul. This heathen doctor thought *he* was God. He was playing with fire; a father's fire. We told him it's not up to him to make that decision.

"You're not God! If that is God's will, so be it." At that time, we felt so alone and weak. "Where is our God? We need him now!"

The phone rang. It was Dr. Mittler, Crystal's original surgeon. He was on his way down and he would meet us in the x-ray room. We were happy to see him. He told us this tumor was a lot larger than the first one and he couldn't guarantee Crystal would survive the operation or become brain damaged.

We told him, "You're not God, and we're not expecting any

promises from you. Our prayers would be that God would guide your hands and His perfect will be done."

This time things were a lot worse. While waiting until the next day for the operation, Crystal was having serious convulsions and none of the staff seemed to be concerned. After yelling for a nurse, they told us convulsions were normal in cases like this. I couldn't buy that answer, seeing Crystal arching up out of bed every time a convulsion would occur. This was serious and scary! It was nothing like the first time.

Crystal was out of it, and we didn't like the condition she was in. Beryl finally called Dr. Mittler to come and see Crystal. When he saw her, he moved up the operation. After several hours of operating, we could finally see her. Dr. Mittler told us the brain tumor was the size of a soft ball and looked like it had been there for a while. When we finally got to go in with Crystal, we noticed she couldn't talk. This really disturbed me, deeply. Just the thought of not hearing her sweet voice again hurt so much. Thankfully, the nurses assured me that in a day or so she would get her voice back.

When coming back to the hospital from work, I walked into Crystal's room. I heard the sweetest words ever spoken to me.

"Hi Dad!"

Fighting back tears, I told her, "It's sure good to see you," as we hugged.

My little girl was now braver than I could ever be. Again, there was an outpouring of visitors, from family members and church family and school friends. Not long after, we took Crystal back home. We picked up our dog, Rosie, at Grandma's and Grandpa's where we had left her for safekeeping. Crystal was sure glad to see her beloved pet. Rosie was also happy Crystal was back home and life would be returning to normal.

When Crystal was well enough to go back to church, she

wanted to visit her friends at the children's ministry called "Just Kidz" at Christ Tabernacle. She wanted to thank all the little children for praying for her, as well as all the leaders in the church. Crystal was a junior helper in an inner city church ministry located in Glendale, Queens, New York.

We would travel fifty miles to this church where God called our family to minister from time to time. God blessed our family with many spiritual gifts and talents, which we wanted to use in serving Him in this unique ministry. Beryl, Nicholas and Crystal all served in the "Just Kidz" ministry. I personally served in the "Sons of God" security ministry, and later, Beryl and I both joined the Christ Tabernacle Choir. If you were ever looking to find the heart and soul of New York City, you would find it at Christ Tabernacle Church.

Our family was blessed to have so much spiritual support from so many great churches. Countless hours of prayer, many meals and financial blessings poured in to help us in our time of need. Crystal lost about a month of school and wanted to catch up with her work. Unfortunately, she had to go through chemotherapy and radiation *again*. That thought made me sick to my stomach, to see my child suffer like that a second time. The treatments were a lot worse than the actual operation. After about a month at home, Crystal was getting stronger, but soon, she was starting to have a bad reaction to the medicine. We took her to the local pediatrician's office, but they didn't have a clue what was going on. There was no time to waste, so we took her to the experts – Schneider Children's Hospital. After they took x-rays, we noticed the technicians, who knew Crystal very well, starting to tear up. My spirit was troubled after seeing that. It was time to start praying. The brain tumor had grown back to its original size in *less than* a month. Chemotherapy needed to be started immediately.

Crystal was very weak at that point. She told me outside the MRI room that as soon as she became well, there were two things she wanted to do: she wanted to join the Christ Tabernacle Youth Choir, and she wanted to return to her

Okinawan Kempo Karate school.

I told her, "That sounds like a plan to me!"

Shortly after the x-ray, Crystal lost her voice again. She looked at me and made a gesture, pointing her fingers toward her eyes, and then pointing her index finger to me as a silent way of saying, "*I got my eye on you, Dad!*"

Everyone she came in contact with told her they loved her, and she would respond that she loves them too, mouthing the words. And then when they would repeat they loved her back, she would say again, "*I love you more.*"

While still in the hospital, Dr. Mittler appeared, and called Beryl and I into a room. He told us there was nothing more that could be done for Crystal. The brain tumor had grown back to its original size and was now interwoven into the brain mesh. This was a problem: there was no way of separating the cancer away from the brain. They also told us Crystal was going to "expire." We told them we still had one more Doctor to consult.

Expire! What a *horrible* word to use regarding my daughter! Then emotional pressure started: the hospital staff thought it best to pull the plug on Crystal. First the doctors, then the social worker badgered us every day. They would always end the uplifting conversation by saying, "*It's your decision.*" This was a 13-year-old! My point of view was that *where there's life, there's still hope!*

That Sunday morning, God sent my pastor, Michael Durso, from the Christ Tabernacle Church, to pray with us. We were all waiting on God; an answer from Heaven was needed. Christians from all over started showing up and praying over her. One of Crystal's sixth grade teachers showed up, Mrs. Deborah Paprocky, to pray over her and began anointing Crystal with oil from Israel. We all were crying to God for a miracle, praying for a healing in Crystal's life. At one point there were people lined up to beg God to heal Crystal.

Crystal slipped into a coma, not able to open her eyes, and then the surgeon told us Crystal's brain had died. The only thing keeping her breathing was the machine. I couldn't believe it. Praying for weeks, up countless nights, unable to raise my voice anymore in prayer, and it was over. *God had taken Crystal to Glory.*

We felt like it was a tugging between the angel of death and us. When it was all over, I was depleted of all my strength. It felt like in my spirit, I had failed Crystal, pleading her case unsuccessfully before Almighty God.

Would God intervene, one last time, while we pulled the life support off Crystal? Or was He going to take her home to Himself? We were all crushed by disappointment. How were we going to continue to live life without her? As Crystal's father, I was always there for her, from when she was born in the delivery room until she slipped into Eternity. Never in my life did I ever feel such deep, emotional pain! From being a fighter, to breaking my pelvis in a terrible car accident in which I was pronounced dead; not one of these near-death events prepared me for what I was now experiencing.

We remembered Crystal at seven years old, when she wanted to run away from home. Her suitcase was packed. And, as she walked out the front door, her mother asked her, "Would you please mail us a post card when you get to where you're going?"

After she walked up the block, we all watched her from the window. She went up the block and she turned around and came back, telling us she missed us. But this time, it was going to be for real. She left and wasn't coming home.

In my heart, I wanted to believe that this was just a nightmare and I'd be waking up soon, but reality was about to set in. One of the hardest decisions we had to make was telling everyone that spent weeks and nights watching over Crystal's bedside that she was gone. *Expired.*

Hours before Crystal lost consciousness and passed into Eternity, she looked at me, her father, knowing I was powerless to help her. She barely had enough strength left, but out of desperation, forced herself to point her two fingers first to her eyes and then her index finger to me. She was letting me know that she's got her eye on me. I did the same back to her. That was our way of agreeing that everything was going to be all right.

Remembering my last communication with Crystal when she could no longer speak, was interpreted by me as meaning *she will be watching us from Heaven.*

All I could think of was the same feeling among us when people heard of the passing of Princess Diana. *Crystal was our Princess, called to Heaven.* God called his young daughter home.

The next painful step in this process was making the arrangements for the wake and a memorial service. Because we left our previous church a year earlier, we were in a terrible position. All our old friends were not around to support us. As word spread, however, there was an overwhelming response. We needed to do something special in celebration of Crystal's life; a life lived for God. We also wanted to thank God for giving us a daughter like Crystal, while she lived on this earth with us. Each moment, day, and year we had with her was to be cherished. Crystal's friends needed closure, too. I could feel their grief and heartbreak. It was unbearable for those young people to suffer such a loss.

Our faith had to be rooted in God's Word in order to go on. Deep in my heart, I prayed that every young friend of hers would accept her leaving for glory as God's perfect will for her life, without casting doubt regarding her illness and not being healed on earth.

We held a wake for two days and had an outpouring of people that came from all over. It was sad to see all her friends crying over her. Crystal had such an impact on everyone. The nurses and the social workers even came from the hospital. At times, there was standing room only. It was amazing to see so many people, young and old, whose lives Crystal had touched.

There was a singer from our home church, Christ Tabernacle, by the name of Calvin Hunt. We had become friends with him. He recorded the song "*We Have Overcome*," with the Christ Tabernacle Choir. We wanted him to come out to Smithtown Gospel Tabernacle, 60 miles from where we were holding the memorial service for Crystal. We wanted to bless our friends and family with a comforting song of hope and joy. Calvin came and sang his song, even though he, himself had just suffered the terrible loss of his own daughter; murdered by her fiancé who had a hidden, sordid past. It was a blessing that he came to minister to us in our grief during his own time of grieving.

The service was incredible. You could feel the Spirit of God moving through the church. We ended by having Calvin singing, "*We Have Overcome by the Blood of the Lamb.*" When it was over, there wasn't a dry eye in the building.

Because of the burial, Crystal's funeral was held on my 50th birthday, November 2, 2005. I knew there would be no joy in celebrating my birthday for some time. In my church, the security team, with whom I served, came out and were pallbearers for Crystal. It was a blessing to see all my co-workers in the ministry honor our family this way. Crystal, Nicholas and Beryl's "Just Kidz" ministry partners came out too.

Many churches and pastors came to show their respect for her. We all hugged and shook hands, and shared tears and stories about Crystal. It was like we were in a bubble. There was a feeling of numbness we were experiencing during that time. The thought in my mind was that after everyone goes back to their life, how many are going to remember my girl, my Crystal?

To our family, it was like a surreal moment in time. My mind wasn't fully comprehending what was happening. There were moments I was still hoping to wake up from a terrible dream, run upstairs and hug my daughter.

As time moved on, the calls, meals, and visits became less and less. But God raised up extraordinary saints in our lives that continued to minister to us. One special person was Marion O' Grady, who was born in County Kerry, Ireland. She always managed to remember everyone's birthdays and special occasions. We were often taken aback to see the Chinese delivery man dropping off dinner sent by Marion. Marion is a Spirit-filled Christian that loves everyone, and decided to adopt our family. Her husband Jay and I share similar interests. We both love working with dog training. Jay also is a very kind, good man. He has become a very dear friend.

In Loving Memory

Of

Crystal Marie Skula

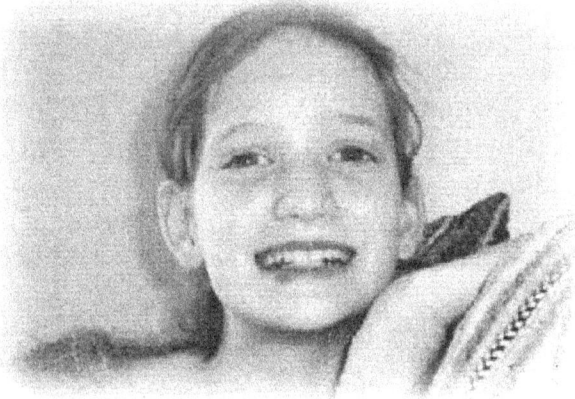

November 23, 1991 - October 25, 2005

O death, where is thy sting? O grave, where is thy victory?
The sting of death is sin; and the strength of sin is the law.
But thanks be to God, which giveth us the victory
through our Lord Jesus Christ.
Therefore, my beloved brethren, be ye stedfast, unmoveable, always
abounding in the work of the Lord, forasmuch as ye know that
your labour is not in vain in the Lord.
1Corinthians 15:55-58

11

THE GRIEVING PROCESS

"Woe is me for my hurt! My wound is grievous; but I said, Truly this is a grief, and I must bear it." –Jeremiah 10:19

My pain and grief after Crystal's death was unbearable. She had been like my shadow, following me everywhere for nearly 14 years. No relief was in sight. I refused to take anti-depressant drugs to numb the pain. The only way to describe it is tearing a piece of your heart out, knowing the rest of your heart can't function without the missing part.

I found the most difficult time was getting up in the morning. The Bible says joy comes in the morning, but it did not for me. Getting up and going through the routines at least kept my focus on my wife and son, who were also struggling and heartbroken.

I wondered if there could *ever* be any healing in my life. In my case, pain had a voice, always calling me to join the misery of my mind. A promise of God needed to come to me in a tangible way. There was such a void and a longing for Eternity. I had always been the strong one in the family, but now I was the weak one. My feelings were bottled up inside of me, with no one to share my pain, except my wife. I felt like crying out loud, but instead I tried to be strong for her and Nick. Often I would think, if only I could have one more day with Crystal. I still wouldn't know how to say good-bye. So we'll just say so-long until we are reunited in eternal glory.

During our grieving, this unanswered question kept coming up: *How do I go on?* I found the answer in a song:

Because He Lives

God sent his son they called him Jesus
He came to love heal and forgive
He lived and died to buy my pardon
An empty grave is there to prove
My Savior lives

Because He lives I can face tomorrow
Because He lives all fear is gone
Because I know He holds the future
And life and is worth the living
Just because He lives

How sweet to hold a newborn baby
And feel the pride and joy he gives
But greater still the calm assurance
This child can face uncertain days
Because he lives

And then one day I'll cross the river
I'll fight life's final war with pain
And then as death gives way to victory
I'll see the lights of glory
And I'll know he lives

Three years later, an unexpected invitation came to us through Crystal's school friends and teachers. We were asked to speak at what would have been Crystal's high school graduation ceremony. Reluctant to accept, we were concerned about putting a damper on the celebration. After seeking God's counsel, I felt in my heart that Crystal's friends needed a final release from their grief. They had to let Crystal go as they stepped into the next phase of their lives. I was inspired to write the following words to them:

Congratulations – you all made it. We want to thank the Lord for this unexpected honor! How can we properly thank the class of 2009 for all your love, prayers and gifts? Our family is humbled this day by all of your compassion and love for Crystal.

We could never find the words to express our love for you. It is a privilege to be asked to stand with so many great Christians, young and old.

I can still remember the first day our family visited Smithtown Christian School. We were considering a Christian education for Nicholas, but Crystal was always quick to recognize an opportunity. As she walked through the foyer she stopped, pulled my arm close and whispered in my ear, "Dad, if Nick doesn't want to come here, I do."

We know the sacrifices that families and teachers have made in supporting this school. An investment has been made in every student here; a spiritual and academic education that will last a lifetime. A standard of excellence has been established.

It is without a doubt that the 2009 graduating class has a special anointing on it. We witnessed a tender spirit of God pour out among its students, we also believe God has equipped this class with greatness to lead and change an out-of-control world to Christ.

You have been assigned the charge! The torch has been passed on to you. Make God Proud. It was your outpouring of love and support for Crystal and our family that helped us weather the storm we weren't prepared for.

A common question people always asked of us is, "How were you able to get through this tragedy?" The answer is found here in this sanctuary. Would everyone look to your left, and now to your right. You just witnessed the power of prayer that has given our family the strength to go on. Your prayers carried us through.

During Crystal's first operation, no one knew what the outcome would be. Just before they rolled Crystal into surgery, we all started to lose control of our emotions. Crystal noticed and told her mother to not be sad, the worse that could happen to her was she'll be with Jesus sooner rather than later. If some of you have ever wondered what the future holds for Crystal, we can tell you this with confidence: When Crystal first walks through Heaven's gates people will know her testimony. Crystal came from a godly heritage and left a godly legacy, which you all are a part of and that still lives on today!

Before this day ends, we want to let you all know our family will always feel connected to all of your lives and we wish you God's speed.

Diane Zarlengo, a dear friend of our family, suggested we join the church choir, since singing would be good therapy for us. Singing all the pain away helped, but there was still a void that couldn't be completely filled. In time, we realized just how much of a profound impact singing did have on our hurting souls. We now had something that could sooth the pain and fill the void. Being made of flesh, I wanted an immediate healing and to stop emotional bleeding. But it would take a grieving *process.*

As years past, there were people who we had lost contact with. Events happened so quickly that there were a lot of people who didn't know what happened to Crystal. One day, a message was left on the answering machine. It was a dear friend of Crystal's named Jocelyn. Jocelyn used to live next door to us, and the two girls played together often. We hadn't heard from their family in quite a while.

The message said, "I have a Christmas present for Crystal and miss her very much. Call me, I want to get together." After hearing this, Beryl and I felt terrible, and decided to go over to their home and break the news of Crystal's death in person.

As we pulled up in their driveway, we could see Jocelyn all excited looking through the window to catch a glimpse of Crystal getting out of the van, to see how much she may have changed over the years. Beryl said it felt like a wound being re-opened; more hurtful than the initial loss. Slowly, we got out of the car and made our way to the front door. The door opened, and now the family was looking past us trying to spot Crystal. They immediately started questioning us as to where she was.

We asked if we could sit down for a moment. There was a sense of seriousness in the air. I took a deep breath to compose myself and explained what had happened.

"Crystal is now with the Lord in Heaven."

There was complete silence. After what felt like a long time, the family slowly started looking toward each other and simultaneously began to sob. They were devastated. They expressed the desire to visit Crystal's grave site. They are from South America and said it's a respectful custom in their culture. We reached out to comfort them. We shared the gospel of Christ with their family. We told them God had given Crystal eternal life and we would all be reunited in Heaven. And, we brought them to visit our church.

Crystal used to babysit for a family up the block from our house; a little boy and his older sister. They loved it when she would watch them. The girl was just a couple of years younger than Crystal and looked up to her. When Crystal left for glory, the little girl's mother didn't want her daughter to view Crystal's body at the funeral service. Her mom thought it would be too traumatic for her daughter. The little girl was never told about what happened to her.

A couple of years later, Nicholas, Beryl and I were raking leaves in our yard, when we noticed a girl on a bicycle had gotten off her bike and was looking around in our yard for Crystal. No one spoke a word to her. You could see a sad look come on her face as she got back on her bike and rode away. She must have guessed what had happened. I wished I would have had some words to minister to her, to ease the pain in that little girl's heart. I am still amazed to see what an impact Crystal has had on so many people.

Beryl, Nick and I decided to go see Crystal's Karate Master, Teruyuki Higa. We were personal friends, and knew he was unaware of Crystal's passing. When Crystal had her first brain operation, Master Higa told Crystal, "Karate girls are not supposed to get sick."

Nick and Crystal studied for years under Master Higa. As the only girl in class, she was a favorite student of his. When we walked through the door his eyes lit up. We had a special relationship with him. As we all took a seat, he smiled but his eyes kept darting toward the door to see when Crystal would walk in and join us. He knew she had survived the first brain surgery. When he asked where Crystal was, we told him. He teared up. This was a hardened man from Okinawa Japan; a rugged, 3-time world karate champion. This was the man who trained us to *never* display any emotion. But Crystal had a profound effect on him, and she had touched even his guarded heart.

Many people would see us in the months after and ask, "Where's Crystal?" It was a painful time. We felt led to get involved in a new ministry called "grief share." The only problem was, *we* were still deeply hurting; *we* were the ones who needed to be ministered to. When you're in ministry for some time, you learn to care for others first, but at times neglect yourself. I am not so sure if that was the right thing to do, but that's all we knew.

Many times people would ask us, "Why didn't God heal Crystal?"

The answer did eventually come to me. There wasn't a doctor or medicine on this earth that could have healed her. Crystal's only chance for healing was going to take place in Heaven. So be it, as the Savior wills.

I thought it would be decades before I'd see her again healed and whole in Heaven; decades until my own passing and journey to meet her there. Then, however, something amazing happened.

12

A JOURNEY TO HEAVEN

"Making request, if by any means now at length I might have a prosperous journey by the will of God to come unto you."
–Romans 1:10

At work, I was trying to keep a smile on my face, yet still struggling emotionally. Even when sitting in church, I just felt pain and sorrow in my heart. As each drawn-out day went by, I couldn't wait until bed time. Without making a sound, I would cry myself to sleep, hoping it would ease the pain. I was trying to hide my emotions from Beryl, thinking it was weakness. Years were passing, and still no relief was in sight.

I was depressed. Things were steadily getting worse; not able to get out of bed and always late to work. The things that once interested me were no longer important to me. If it wasn't for my wife and son, I would have asked God to just take me home, too.

One night, after sobbing for a long time, I had fallen into a deep sleep. I felt a restful peace come upon me as if I were going into a coma, sinking into my pillow. There seemed to be a loss of consciousness. I was no longer able to make decisions and felt a spinning sensation. Then I saw a bright light flash, causing me to open my eyes. The flash was like when an old fashioned camera light-bulb would go off, blinding you for a moment, and then making you see spots. When my eyes cleared and my vision refocused, I was able to see things for miles: every detail. Even though I was not able to speak a word, my hearing was very clear.

Where was I? I found myself in the middle of a large, happy crowd of people. Something I'd never felt before was in the atmosphere; something unexplainable. Every time I took a breath, it was like I became stronger. Something was feeding my spirit. There was such a clean and fresh fragrance, too, like a summer rain.

What is this place?

The reality of what was happening dawned on me; I was in *Heaven*. As I scanned the excited crowd, I didn't recognize anyone. A feeling of loneliness hit me, until I saw my wife Beryl. I hugged her, and we felt we had finally made it home!

Now it was time to find *Crystal*. Working our way through the crowd, there she was, making her way toward us! Tears of joy were starting to flow. She stood out in the midst of everyone. It was like she had become a crown jewel of Heaven. In amazement, we always knew the greatness of God, but never imagined this kind of restoration.

A desire to find the Lord in this crowd was pressing my soul. "My God, where are You?" I needed to bow before the Almighty and thank Him. A spirit of love had taken over my soul. His promises were true all along, from the beginning of time and into Eternity. Words spoken from God on earth had now turned into a living reality I was experiencing.

Finally, Crystal made it over to us. She grabbed her mother's hand and started pulling us away from the crowd. This troubled me. I wondered w*hy wasn't she taking the time to hug and kiss us hello?* In my strength, I tried to stop her to embrace her as she continued to pull us along. Crystal had a power we hadn't received yet.

When we got to the end of the greeting room, we entered a larger, empty room where a man was beating a drum. It appeared to me like he was summoning everyone into this area. Still being pulled along by Crystal, she led us to a tremendous altar platform. After looking at the platform, I noticed three people sitting there. My eyes couldn't focus on them, but everything else was clear. Was it the Lord Himself? When I turned to Crystal to ask her who they were, there was no voice in me able to speak. When trying to embrace my daughter, my body was frozen. All I was able to do was *see* and *hear*. If God was there, in my spirit I felt it was better if I waited to look upon the Holy of Holies until He spoke to *me*. So turning to Crystal, I studied her and compared her from the last time I had seen her.

She now had a godly glow the Lord had given her. All of her beautiful hair was restored. That earthly doctor's diagnosis wasn't true in Heaven. The Doctor of Heaven is perfect in all His ways. Not even a scar from the operation was left. She seemed to know that I was staring at her, examining her restored beauty. As she was looking to the altar, thanking God, she smiled, knowing all the Lord had done for her.

Crystal was dressed in a gleaming, white ballerina outfit. She was the only one dressed like that. There was a sense of concern, being her earthly father, wanting to protect her from people seeing her as different, but she *was* different. Crystal was now doing toe lifts. She was loosening her leg muscles, as taught by me, as a way to stretch herself to get ready for strenuous activity. I saw Crystal softly bite her lower lip. She would always do that when she was nervous. I doubt she was really nervous or stiff, but it may have been a sign to me saying, "Watch me, Dad I'm going to make you proud of me. God is going to use me to give a special blessing, just for you."

Not knowing what to expect next, I noticed this large room had filled up. Crystal had a group of young kids who seemed to be watching her every move intently. There appeared to be some kind of connection with them. The atmosphere was changing, and there was a sense of anticipation, of something great about to take place.

Were we waiting for God to speak? Instead came a song. At first, I didn't recognize it, but then it hit me...I know this song. We sang it in the choir at church: "*He Rejoices Over Me*" written by Pastor Steven Carey, sung by his wife, Mary. The song was a perfectly tailored, life story of Crystal's struggle here on this earth: suffering through many operations, losing her hair, memory loss, as well as strength being drained from her with each treatment. The song's lyrics went like this:

Once I was singing a sorrowful song
Sadness, despair all around
Looking to some for encouragement
Seeking, but none could be found

But when I was seeking; the Father sought me
Saw me in my need
Lifted me up from my desperation
Now He celebrates my salvation
He rejoices over me

He celebrates with singing
By the song of the Lamb
And His grace I've been set free
He rejoices over me

Now while the instruments were playing the song's intro, it started to sound like the movie theme from the *Lion King*. Crystal started running very fast toward the stage and leaped high in the air, while spinning wildly. The entire audience tensed up as they saw that she had overestimated her distance and set herself up for a crash landing. Her body movement and speed were just too aggressive. But in Crystal's graceful fashion, her landing was perfect. The audience let out a gasp of relief. All those young people started cheering, going crazy, and yelling, "*Go daughter of God, bring Him GLORY!*"

Crystal was now worshiping God in dance. She was leaping and bouncing all over the stage, dancing before God Almighty. By this time, other ballerinas appeared to join in the dance along with her. I was just sobbing. Crystal may have not been able to dance in the Nutcracker ballet, but to worship God in dance was so much more incredible! I was telling everyone around me, "That's my daughter." In my spirit, I said, "Hey, wait a minute! I am able to talk now!"

Now, thinking I had regained some of my abilities, I was determined to get my overdue hug. But just as I set my sights on her to move towards her through the crowd, my voice was gone again. And when I blinked my eyes, everything disappeared.

I woke up in my dark, silent bedroom. There was a feeling of frustration, wanting to return to the vision with Crystal, but immediately there remained a strong sense of excitement within my soul. God had taken me to a place in my spirit where I had never been before, but where Crystal was *now*. God had placed a piece of Heaven in my soul to hold me at peace until we will meet again. When I told my wife what had happened, I was expecting a reaction of disbelief, but she received it as a comfort; a gift from God to help me with my grief.

I now know this to be true:

A moment in Heaven in the presence of God is worth more than a thousand years on earth! Heaven is a place where God takes shattered dreams and brings them back to life again.

To be continued...Revelation 21:5

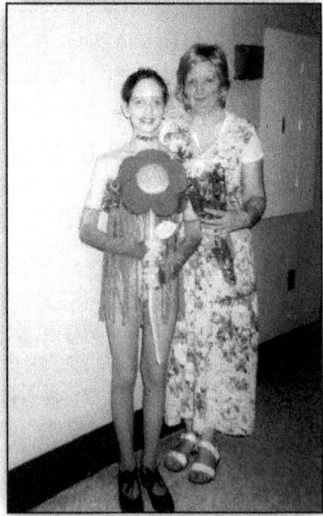

DEDICATIONS

Dear Beloved Reader,

When asked many times, "How did you get through the trial of our daughter's battle with brain cancer?" my answer is always the same; "By the grace of God, I will carry on."

I would pray, and during those difficult times when I could scarcely lift my voice in prayer, I would listen to praise music. As it says in the Holy Bible, *God inhabits the praises of His people.*

(Zechariah 2:10) I could feel the Lord's loving arms around me and He has carried me through those times of sadness. *I am comforted by the One who comforts.* (John 14:16)

When someone would say "We are sorry for your loss," we would reply, "We have lost nothing."
For whatsoever you bind on Earth shall be bound in Heaven, and whatsoever you loose on Earth shall be loosed in Heaven. What this passage means to us is that we have her new address, which is in Heaven. (John 14:2)

Our dear daughter, Crystal, is always on my mind and in my heart. She was such a joy! God gave our daughter the confidence of Jesus Christ, so that she was able to face her battle with grace, dignity, and courage.

To God be the glory!

In His love,

Beryl Skula
Crystal's Mom

Dedication to Nicholas III

One unsung hero in this story is our only son Nicholas. My faithful and loyal son endured a lot of suffering at the young age of 18. He was unable to physically do anything to help his little sister; he could only watch and pray. After days became weeks at the hospital, Nicholas volunteered to stay home by himself to take care of Rosie, the family dog, who Crystal loved very much.

While at Crystal's bedside, my mind and heart began hurting for Nicholas. He needed to be here. Crystal idolized Nicholas and was inspired by her brother. He always made her laugh. As they got older, there was very little disagreement between them. We were all praying that God would miraculously heal Crystal from her sick bed and that we would walk out of the hospital arm-in-arm. When God revealed His will to take her home, our emotions weren't prepared to accept the loss of her presence.

I remember observing Nicholas' reaction to this. He seemed to swallow his grief, and he never shed a tear in public. In a surprising moment, Nicholas received a joy from the Lord that filled his heart with peace. My little man, who I brought into this world, had grown into a giant of a man. While he lives on this earth, he will have to remember there will be eternity for him to spend with his sister.

My soul is well knowing that my son has developed a great faith in God. When my turn comes to stand before God, I am looking forward to my Maker saying these words; *"Well done, thou good and faithful servant,"* and Nicholas and Crystal will come to mind. Nicholas will be a living testimony on this earth that his parents didn't compromise; they lived God's way.

Thank you, son. Love,
Dad

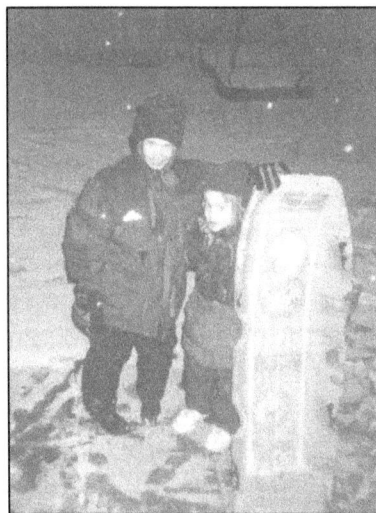

Dedication from Nicholas III

My father dedicated several years to completing this book. We all felt it would be appropriate to contribute as a family so I will share some thoughts on my sister, Crystal. I recall first seeing her at the hospital the day she was born. There was a large, pink room with a huge, glass window. I had a thrill of excitement, knowing my sister was behind the window. I stood on my tip toes to see in. I pushed my little body as high as I could, held the window's ledge with my hands, and peered in as a climber ascending the peak of a mountain. Rows of babies lined the room, and there she was - my baby sister!

As time went on, that baby grew up, and determined as ever, she went through life. Always following and imitating me, she never let her age inhibit her. She wanted to do whatever I did. Not only that, but she would do it *better*. She always had to be first to be ready for school. I remember one time I was "sleeping" on the couch before the bus came. She ran down the stairs exclaiming, "I'm first! I beat you getting ready!" However, I had used the blanket to conceal the fact was already dressed and ready to go. I had pulled one over on her: I was ready first. She was mad as a hornet, and made sure to get up even earlier from then on. If I played the recorder, she would play clarinet *and* piano. Her constant playing was very annoying and I would always complain. To escape the noise, I'd go outside to play with my friends. But sure enough, who followed right behind me? Crystal.

Siblings share a special bond, and being the older one carries a responsibility to be there and look out for the younger ones. They look up to you and mimic the things you do; good and bad. I made sure I was a good role model to my sister, and it was a mantle I gladly took on. Reading the book for the first time brought back many good memories of my sister. As you read this book, I hope you enjoyed the many stories about the precious life of my sister, Crystal.

Nicholas Skula III

To the Memory of The Reverend Calvin Hunt

To a man that had become a broken vessel, in a hopeless situation, never expecting a God in Heaven to hear his cries of despair, but in a moment of desperation a visitation from the Savior changed his life forever.

No longer broken, his life was made whole, once again. Through God's love, he poured out a godly greatness only for those new and clean vessels.

Now completely faithful and true; there was a new life to be lived to please God. With an urgency in his heart, Calvin had an excitement to help other broken vessels escape from living a life of hell here on earth. There was a burning need to let the lost taste the goodness of heaven while on earth.

Calvin's new commission was clear: restoring others through the saving knowledge of Jesus Christ to the fullness of God. Calvin's only regret about leaving this world was leaving so many unsaved souls apart from God.

Entrusting his ministry work to the familiar voices of his family and loved ones left behind, he was convinced that the many vessels he once ministered to would be taken care of.

With God's greatness around us, we must remember what our Lord allows us to see in men. God's Spirit worked through a once broken vessel; God anointed him and brought a greatness to work through the man, Calvin Hunt.

Your friend in Christ,

Nicholas J. Skula

LETTERS/NOTES FROM FRIENDS & FAMILY

Poem written by Eleanor Skula, Crystal's Grandmother:

CRYSTAL

I have a pretty granddaughter, she has gone so far from me
She left the ones who love her - her precious family

I know Dear Lord Your will is best, though we at times say no
I found it oh so hard to finally let her go

I know your will and plan for us is best and very fair
But Dear Lord I miss her so, my Crystal with long blond hair

Her big blue eyes that lighted up, when we played and had
such fun
You saw the love that we both shared and whispered Crystal
"Come"

Your arms Dear Lord were opened wide for her to sit and rest
I found it hard to let her go and knew that you know best

I wonder what she says and does to God who loves her all day

long
I'd like to think she's in His choir and singing Him a song

So until then I'll watch and wait for time to hurry by
When Jesus calls I'll meet you there with joy up in the sky

I love you more,

Grandma
Eleanor Skula
June 2009

Poem written by Carin Cheng:

LIFE TO YEARS

Having a diagnosis of cancer,
The doctors gave me their answer.
The pain was a tumor inside.
It was in the Lord, I had to abide.

The shock was enormous, cancer for life.
My mind filled with sadness, regret and strife.
This is too much for me to bear.
Christ on the cross, who can compare?

Oh for the joy, He endured the pain,
Oh for the love, He removed our stain.
On to Sloan Kettering: my doctor did tests,
Hopes were high and we hoped for the best.

The news was not hopeful, but pretty grim,
An aggressive tumor taking vigor and vim.
Well, "How long do you say I have to live?
Be honest and direct, what hope to you give?"

"Months to years" my doctor did say.
My eyes opened wide in shock and dismay.
"Years...how many? One, two, seven?"
"Less," he said, and I thought of heaven.

I sought the Lord, and He told me, "Don't fret, don't fear,
What is a month, what is a year?
They say months to years. I say
Years to life. Don't dismay."

No more sorrow, no more pain,
Then outside I heard the rain.
My tears welled up as they sometimes do
I said, "Lord, You know I trust in You."

Cleansing tears, they wash me clean.

Letter from Marissa Miller

I met Crystal in 5th grade. At first, I was envious of her because everyone loved her so much. When I got to know her, I realized why. Crystal was an amazing girl and an amazing friend. She always cared for everyone around her. She could always tell when something was wrong and knew how to cheer you up. Crystal is one of my best friends and in my heart she will always be! Crystal was always so happy and full of energy. Crystal loved sugar and used to tell me, "Life's too short...eat dessert first!" Of course she would be bouncing off the walls later. People always say, "Remember the happy times." but with Crystal that is all you had.

In eighth grade we were on the same late bus coming home from soccer practice. Every day we would talk and have fun. We used to wave to the cars behind us and see how many people would wave back. We would just laugh and laugh.

That summer, Crystal came to the beach with us. We were soooo mature. We built sand castles and buried each other in the sand. We collected seashells along the shoreline just because we could. These are the kind of happy days I will always remember.

Crystal had a lot of pain in her life but she was always so strong. She loved God so much, and we can know she is with the Lord right now and her pain is forgotten. We will all miss her. What's not to miss? I know I will see her again. We will be together again without the sadness and pain. I will never forget Crystal Skula. She has touched my life, as she has many others. It was sad to see her go, but I know she is happy now and I will see her again!!!

I LOVE YOU CRYSTAL!!!

Your forever friend...
Marissa Miller

More Memories from Marissa Miller

I remember Crystal's big sleepover birthday party when the large group of girls all went to the movie theater to see the SpongeBob Movie. We then came home and played Life and watched *Ella Enchanted* which was my gift to her. We snooped through Nick's room and found a gas mask and probably about a million dollars in change scattered about the room. It was like a piggy bank exploded or something. We all watched home videos of Crystal as an adorable child doing karate just like her beloved SpongeBob. We had lots of fun playing with Crystal's face paint only to discover that it was very hard to wash off. Somehow we discovered that toothpaste would wash it off.

Although nobody else remembers it, I remember we had a dress down day and she came in wearing a shirt with Fruit

Loops all over it and the moment I saw that shirt I got excited. I thought that was the coolest thing ever. And she loved Limited Too. I still have a Frisbee from there that she gave to me for a part of a birthday gift one year. In sixth grade she and I used to sit on the bean bag chairs together during free time and draw pictures on the white boards, writing secret messages to each other. She came to the beach with my mom, my little brother Brandon and I once. That was such a great day. Brandon, Crystal and I played in the sea and sand for hours.

One thing everybody knew about Crystal was her love of sugar. I think brownies and ice cream were her two favorites. She would buy ice cream from the cafeteria all the time. Brownies were more for special occasions like parties. Kristy's mom always made brownies and that was something she appreciated more than everybody else. Crystal was the first student to discover that the chicken nuggets from the cafeteria bounce when you drop them. She was so excited to show everybody. Her favorite lunch from the cafeteria was chicken patty day. She would draw smiley faces on the chicken with her ketchup and only referred to them as "Crabby Patties" in honor of SpongeBob.

I always found it funny that teachers thought Crystal was a calm quiet girl but that was all they really saw of her. In class, Crystal was shy. If she was called on or the teacher was talking to her for whatever reason, Crystal would get all quiet. She did this little squinty thing with her eyes and her voice would be a little shaky and I could tell she was nervous. That is the side that the teachers saw. They did not see the other side of Crystal that all our friends loved. The teachers did not know that Crystal could be wild and crazy. She could be spontaneous and energetic but she was always kind and generous. Crystal always had a smile and laughs were easy to come by. She was the first to volunteer to play pranks on me when at a sleepover at Kristy's when I was the last one to wake up. She was the first to think of a game to play on the late bus on the way home from soccer. She was the first to tell a ridiculous joke and make it funny when nobody else could. She had so much fun in everything she did. It was obvious in everything that she did that the joy and peace she constantly radiated came straight from God.

I also remember her saying her famous motto "Life is short; eat dessert first!" One time she said it at lunch after we found out about the cancer and she was back in school after being hospitalized. It really went deep into my heart when she said it that time, and I cry as I think about it, because she knew all along that her life would be short, even though she expressed it in a happy and silly way. When she said it that time, I really became sad as I remembered how close she came to dying and how blessed she was to still be alive. I thought about her motto seriously for the first time, and it has a new meaning for me.

Thoughts from Megan Mohr

Crystal was someone who I admired. She was the happiest person I knew even though she went through the most hardships. She persevered through trial after trial, but she still found joy! Crystal knew that God was going to use her life for His glory and she gave her life wholeheartedly. Even though Crystal was only with us for a short time, she lived life to the fullest and experienced more joy than many people do in their lifetime.

Megan Mohr

More Memories from Megan Mohr

Crystal and Marissa always had a great time annoying Jeanette by taking a little bit of every food that they could find and mixing it all together...Jeanette would get so grossed out.

She would always laugh about it with Crystal and Marissa later though.

Once, Crystal brought a can of spray cheese for her lunch. She sprayed it all over the table so that she could laugh about it. IT was such a "Crystal" thing to do. She made us smile. Like when she brought a pair of big clown shoes to school. That was fun. Crystal was great to have at parties, especially birthday parties. If there was a cake, and Crystal was going to have some (which she always did) either she would stick her face in her piece or she would somehow manage to get it all over her face some other way. She loved making fun messes with other things as well, though. Once at one of Alanna's parties, we were all coloring Easter eggs and Crystal got the dye all over her skin. She had some difficulty getting it off, but that only added to the fun for her.

I remember at every birthday party Crystal would feel the need to mush her face in the cake. Her eyes and nose would be completely covered with cake. She would always walk around for at least 15 minutes with cake on her face. She would look so funny and it would always make me laugh.

It was graduation day for eighth graders, and the whole class was waiting in the gym. I walked in and Crystal came over and she told me she thought her dress looked too young. The only thing I remember is hugging her and making sure she felt beautiful, because she looked gorgeous that day.

The most memorable time I had with Crystal was her birthday party. That day was the day I met a new friend, Marissa Barasso, and it was such a great party. I remember going to the new Spongebob movie and Crystal getting thirteen boxes of brownies for her birthday. I think I went to bed around 5:00 a.m. talking to Marissa, Alanna, and Crystal. Crystal was the first one of us to fall asleep. That night was the latest I stayed up and is still the latest I have every stayed up.

Every day during lunch, her favorite meal from the lunchroom was chicken patty. But, of course, Crystal would call it Crabby Patty. She would have ice cream every day and when eating it she would say, "Eat dessert first." I remember going to Alanna's birthday party, and we decided to color Easter eggs. Crystal made the biggest mess and her fingers were dyed a blueish purple color. The whole party, she was hugging a Spongebob piñata.

We went to Six Flags for the sixth grade field trip. During lunch, Crystal took straws and put them in her nose. Then she started making noises like a walrus. Then Alanna join in and made walrus sounds with her. It was a very entertaining lunch.

Letter from Kristy Roman

Fifth Grade:
One time at lunch Crystal paid 50 cents to buy a bag of gushers. I saw them and asked her for one. She gave me the whole bag out of her overwhelmingly generous spirit. As she watched me eat them, her sweet tooth was activated and she just HAD to have one. She offered me a dollar for just one gusher, even though she could have bought two more whole packets for that amount of money. During fifth grade, Crystal also taught us the "Comet" song. I don't know what it's from, but these are the lyrics: "Comet: some Comet, and vomit today!" I tried to direct a "big production" based on this song at recess. I lined up Kristen, Megan, Jeanette, Alanna, Crystal, and myself on the bleachers with everyone's places and cues. Even though it was the first year I met Crystal, we were close enough for me to invite her to my 11th birthday party. She brought the present into school with her and I could see some gray fur sticking out of the top of the gift bag. She said, "I hope you like dogs," totally giving away the surprise! I still have it on my bed. I think of her whenever I see it.

Sixth Grade:

Crystal LOVED SpongeBob. For one of my birthdays she gave me a weird Spongebob set in which you make the background out of this weird goo. I still have the Spongebob and Patrick that came with it. At Alanna's party, she and Kristen fought and Crystal wanted to marry it. For Crystal's 13th birthday we went to see the Spongebob Squarepants movie. I gave her thirteen boxes of brownies as her present because I knew that was her favorite! A week later she sent me a thank-you note saying she had 7 boxes left. I still have the card.

Seventh Grade:

It was the day of the Thanksgiving Feast in seventh grade. My mom had told me to get some of everything because she was going to come in to school and would eat what I didn't want. As I was coming to the table with my tray, I saw my mom hovering over Crystal saying, "Why didn't you get yams?" I was embarrassed of her and said, "Mom, leave her alone. She can get whatever she wants." My mom turned around in surprise, shocked at the sight of me. She looked at Crystal's face and said, "Oh I thought you were Kristy!" She said we looked the same from the back because Crystal's wig was the same color as my hair.

Letter from Kristen Ciercirski

Wow, the memories I've had of Crystal. She loved ice cream and she loved Spongebob. I remember that she loved the Spongebob piñata at Alanna's party that one year. I loved her hair. She gave me the Tomagachi game that I still have. We used to walk to the laundromat and walk around in there. We used to slide on the ice outside her house and play with Rosie outside in the backyard. She always said Rosie only spoke German. She was my best friend. We used to think everything was funny. We used to draw pictures. We also made a black sparkly volcano together for a project in sixth grade. She liked Anthony and sent him a rose for Valentine's Day, but was too shy and she took it from the delivery person before Anthony would find out about it.

She loved the French fries from the school cafeteria and brownies. She played with the little kid in the hospital by hiding behind toy food. She absolutely loved my niece Sabrina, and whenever she came over she would have to hold her. She also loved my dog, Mr. Parker and Alanna's dog, Sammy. She used to always eat Mallomars. They were so good.

Thoughts from Jeanette Olish

I remember having fun with Crystal and her church friends when she took me to Awana one night. I also remember how much my dog loved her. From the moment Crystal first met Buddy he was attached to her.

Letter from Alanna Foerth

I remember Crystal always being happy and smiling and trying to make sure that everyone else around her was happy. Every time I picture her face she is smiling, because it was a rare occasion for her not to smile. One of the memories I have of her is with the Spongebob piñata that I got for one of my birthday parties. My mom got it but never got candy for it. Crystal of course, loving Spongebob as much as she did became obsessed with it. She took it all around the house and sometimes she would kiss it. The next year, for some reason, she stuck holes in it with a pencil. I still have it. She was always entertaining us and there was never a dull moment around her. I remember the time that she took me to the circus with her family and they had box seats. Of course, she ate a ton of junk food there. Her motto for life was "Life is short, eat dessert first!" She really lived it out, not just by eating dessert, but by having fun all the time.

CRYSTAL MARIE SKULA MEMORIAL FOUNDATION

Dear Readers and Friends of Crystal,

Thank you for your support. We hope you were blessed to see God's work through this young lady's amazing life. Now that Crystal resides in the Kingdom of Heaven, we that remain would like to keep her godly legacy alive. We would like to encourage young people to live for God and choose his path for their lives.

We also realize that there are many hurting people who have lost their loved ones. They have many questions and much grief to bear. Our family has been involved in sharing their pain and trying to comfort the hurting.

When a loved one passes after a long battle such as cancer or sickness, there are financial needs. The Skula family was blessed to have so many caring people to help us with the needs we faced. Many families don't have that kind of support.

If God leads you to send a financial gift of any amount you can afford, we would be able to help the needs of people in difficult times and ease the pain. Please write to us and share your story; we would like to hear from you.

Attn: Crystal Marie Skula Memorial
P.O. Box 240
Islip Terrace, N.Y. 11752

In God's Love,
Nicholas & Beryl Skula

ABOUT THE AUTHOR

Nicholas Skula Jr., a native New Yorker, was born an eternal optimist. When asked, Nicholas will tell you his inspiration comes from God and from growing up in church. He has dedicated his adult life to serving God. His love for singing gospel music inspired Nick and his wife Beryl to join the award-winning Christ Tabernacle Choir, based in Glendale, Queens, New York. This choir is known for touring the country, singing on television, and ministering in prisons. The gospel album *Change the Atmosphere* earned the choir a Dove Award. Nicholas has also been involved with his church's outreach teams, ministering to countless intercity youth.

Tragedy struck Nicholas when his thirteen year old daughter lost her battle with brain cancer. He relied on his faith in Jesus Christ, his personal Lord and Savior, to get him through.

Nicholas was inspired to write *He Rejoices Over Me* to comfort to those who also have suffered a similar loss.

SPEAKER PAGE

Nick and Beryl Skula desire to minister to and impact the lives of others through sharing their story of love, loss and hope with those who are grieving.

If you know of a school, organization, church, or community in need of powerful speakers for events, memorials or outreach, please consider connecting with the Skula family.

To connect with the Skulas about speaking and ministry opportunities, please contact them at the following:

Email: **Boro3154@live.com**

Address: **Crystal Marie Skula Memorial**
P.O. Box 240
Islip Terrace, N.Y. 11752

Online: **www.HeRejoicesOverMe.com**

He Rejoices Over Me is proudly published by:

Creative Force Press
Guiding Aspiring Authors to Release Their Dream

www.CreativeForcePress.com

Do You Have a Book in You?

www.ingramcontent.com/pod-product-compliance
Lightning Source LLC
LaVergne TN
LVHW051240080426
835513LV00016B/1690